Cambridge Elements

Elements in Law, Economics and Politics
edited by
Series Editor in Chief
Carmine Guerriero, *University of Bologna*
Series Co-Editors
Alessandro Riboni, *École Polytechnique*
Jillian Grennan, *Duke University, Fuqua School of Business*
Petros Sekeris, *TBS Education*

US INNOVATION INEQUALITY AND TRUMPISM

The Political Economy of Technology Deserts in a Knowledge Economy

Victor Menaldo
University of Washington

Nicolas Wittstock
University of Washington

Shaftesbury Road, Cambridge CB2 8EA, United Kingdom

One Liberty Plaza, 20th Floor, New York, NY 10006, USA

477 Williamstown Road, Port Melbourne, VIC 3207, Australia

314–321, 3rd Floor, Plot 3, Splendor Forum, Jasola District Centre, New Delhi – 110025, India

103 Penang Road, #05–06/07, Visioncrest Commercial, Singapore 238467

Cambridge University Press is part of Cambridge University Press & Assessment, a department of the University of Cambridge.

We share the University's mission to contribute to society through the pursuit of education, learning and research at the highest international levels of excellence.

www.cambridge.org
Information on this title: www.cambridge.org/9781009461498

DOI: 10.1017/9781009461450

© Victor Menaldo and Nicolas Wittstock 2025

This publication is in copyright. Subject to statutory exception and to the provisions of relevant collective licensing agreements, no reproduction of any part may take place without the written permission of Cambridge University Press & Assessment.

When citing this work, please include a reference to the DOI 10.1017/9781009461450

First published 2025

A catalogue record for this publication is available from the British Library

ISBN 978-1-009-46149-8 Hardback
ISBN 978-1-009-46146-7 Paperback
ISSN 2732-4931 (online)
ISSN 2732-4923 (print)

Cambridge University Press & Assessment has no responsibility for the persistence or accuracy of URLs for external or third-party internet websites referred to in this publication and does not guarantee that any content on such websites is, or will remain, accurate or appropriate.

US Innovation Inequality and Trumpism

The Political Economy of Technology Deserts in a Knowledge Economy

Elements in Law, Economics and Politics

DOI: 10.1017/9781009461450
First published online: January 2025

The three co-editors in charge of Menaldo's element were: Carmine Guerriero, Petros Sekeris and Alessandro Riboni.

Victor Menaldo
University of Washington

Nicolas Wittstock
University of Washington

Author for correspondence: Victor Menaldo, vmenaldo@uw.edu

Abstract: President Trump embraced economic populism centered on trade protectionism, restrictions on international capital and technology flows, and subsidies for American raw material providers and domestic manufacturers. More innovative US counties roundly rejected this economic paradigm: Voters in innovation clusters of all sizes and across the country repudiated Trumpism in both 2016 and 2020. Trump's tariffs and attacks on global supply chains, restrictions on visas for skilled foreign workers, and his overall hostility toward high-tech sectors threatened the innovative firms that motor these places' economies. Trump was different in degree but not kind from previous American populists such as Jennings Bryan and Perot: They too exploited innovation inequality, but were less successful because, before the digital revolution, the industrial organization of American technological progress was not rooted in vertically disintegrated global supply chains. Thus, populism may not only be about resentment toward elites and experts but threaten innovation.

This Element also has a video abstract: Cambridge.org/ELEP_Menaldo

Keywords: Trump, trade protectionism, innovation, political polarization, economic populism

© Victor Menaldo and Nicolas Wittstock 2025

ISBNs: 9781009461498 (HB), 9781009461467 (PB), 9781009461450 (OC)
ISSNs: 2732-4931 (online), 2732-4923 (print)

Contents

1. Introduction: Trumpism's Take on Innovation — 1
2. Contextualizing Trumpism as Populism — 14
3. Geography of Trumpism in 2016 — 22
4. Theoretical Framework — 25
5. Why Less Innovation Equals Support for Trumpism — 31
6. Setting the Stage to Test the Theoretical Framework's Implications — 36
7. Causal Relationship between Innovation and Trumpism, 2016 — 52
8. Innovation, President Trump, and the 2020 Elections — 79
9. The Historical Roots of Innovation Inequality and Populism — 95
10. Reflections on Populism and Polarization — 115

References — 120

1 Introduction: Trumpism's Take on Innovation

> Some in liberal-leaning Silicon Valley ... derided Trump in 2016 as a Luddite unfit for public office in an age when questions about self-driving cars and cancer cures no longer seem the distant stuff of science fiction. To the policy wonks of Washington, Trump's greatest sin wasn't just his abrogation of technology – many of his voters shared his digital reluctance anyway. Rather, it was Trump's absent science or technology agenda and his missing complement of aides advising him on the issues (Romm 2017).

During the campaign trail in 2016, Candidate Trump espoused economic nationalism that repackaged earlier versions of American populism. Trump pitted ordinary Americans against a "corrupt" elite who he blamed for all manner of social and economic ills. Besides railing against illegal immigration, he campaigned against Chinese and Mexican imports (see, for example, Diamond 2016) and decried American trade deficits and international supply chains (Trump 2016b). He championed restrictions on international capital and technological flows and teased big subsidies for both US raw material producers and domestic suppliers in heavy manufacturing if he got elected. Trump advocated industrial policies to revive mature or declining sectors such as steel, fossil fuel-powered vehicles, coal, and oil.

Correspondingly, he said little about basic science, research and development (R&D), and education. If anything, Trump expressed hostility toward technologically dynamic sectors, especially so-called Big Tech firms. In short, he spoke the language of semi-trucks, not semiconductors. Trump then followed through with many of his populist economic promises during his presidency, starting a trade war with China, renegotiating the North American Free Trade Agreement (NAFTA), and even imposing tariffs on America's European allies.

Fast-forward to July 2021, when the US Senate passed the Innovation and Competition Act during President Biden's first year in office. It pledged investments of more than $110 billion in the American semiconductor industry, the National Science Foundation (NSF), the Department of Energy (DOE), regional technology hubs, and the 5G wireless network.[1] It vowed to help the United States improve the development and commercialization of AI, quantum computing, biotechnology, and advanced energy.[2]

---

[1] In February 2022, the US House of Representatives passed a companion bill, the America COMPETES Act, to, among other things, subsidize American semiconductor chip manufacturing, increase spending on scientific research and R&D, and promote international trade. In July 2022, the component of the bill subsidizing US semiconductors was put into a separate bill.

[2] This law provides roughly $280 billion in new funding for domestic research and the manufacturing of semiconductors in the United States.

During his 2020 presidential campaign, candidate Biden had spoken, quite often, about the need to revive American leadership in public R&D and promote technological development.[3] He promised substantial increases in green energy R&D, which were eventually enshrined in the Inflation Reduction Act in 2022.[4] Biden also promised funding for other "breakthrough technologies" such as Artificial Intelligence (AI) and quantum computing, and made the case for increased support for start-ups, incubators, and innovation hubs. And he spoke about enhancing broadband infrastructure and making increased public investments in the 5G network.[5] Biden pledged well over $300 billion for these initiatives.[6]

Had he secured reelection in 2020, it seems unlikely that a second-term Trump presidency would have championed similar policies focused on science, technology, and innovation.[7] His brand of trade protectionism, threats to global supply chains, and antipathy toward immigration, including that of skilled foreign workers who are usually employed by innovative American firms to help them compete globally, seemed to presage a slower pace of technological development in dynamic sectors, especially regarding the internet of things (IOT) and AI (Deng, Delios, and Peng 2020). Trump's record on education, basic scientific research, R&D, and green energy was roundly lambasted by the high-tech community (Lapowsky 2018; O'Mara 2022).

Unsurprisingly, therefore, a long parade of high-tech firms' leaders congratulated Joe Biden in effusive terms after he won the 2020 presidential election, with many praising his campaign promises around education, immigration, and digital infrastructure (see Palmer 2020).

Even though Biden was clearly the preferred candidate of more innovative areas, however, he co-opted some of President Trump's economic agenda, especially policies aimed at voters in the Battleground States of Michigan, Pennsylvania, and Wisconsin (Barret 2020; Hull 2020). These previous Democratic Party strongholds,

---

[3] This paragraph draws extensively on Atkinson et al. (2020).

[4] The law includes $370 billion in spending on energy and climate change, expands clean energy tax credits for wind, solar, nuclear, clean hydrogen, clean fuels, and carbon capture, and makes it easier to claim a tax credit for clean vehicles.

[5] These promises were delivered in the form of the $1 trillion infrastructure bill, which Biden signed into law in November 2021. It includes provisions to broaden access to broadband, provide electric vehicle charging stations, and enhance cybersecurity.

[6] Once elected president, Biden further signaled his commitment to R&D by including record spending on science and technology in each of his budgets, including for both basic and applied research. He also proposed funding for the new Directorate for Technology, Innovation, and Partnerships within the NSF, which focuses on the commercialization of new technologies, and for ARPA-H, which is dedicated to health research.

[7] Three exceptions were his support for increasing R&D in AI and quantum computing, as well as US semiconductor manufacturing, and providing greater internet and wireless coverage in rural areas (see Atkinson et al. 2020).

also known as Blue Wall states, helped launch Trump into power in 2016 (Clark 2017; McQuarrie 2017).[8]

Much has been said about the reasons why Trump flipped those states from the Democrats vis-à-vis the 2012 presidential election and why Biden flipped them back from President Trump in 2020. Explanations as to why they were up for grabs in the first place and how the election winner was able to placate their restless voters range from making successful appeals to rural consciousness to addressing anxiety about industrial decay to exploiting educational differences, and race or demographic change. Indeed, Judis and Teixeira (2023) and Ruffini (2023) suggest that Republicans have successfully appealed to voters in post-industrial areas who feel left behind by the Democratic Party's policies, which voters blame for unemployment, reduced income levels, and the hollowing out of manufacturing due to cheap Chinese imports or automation.

To our knowledge, researchers have not systematically explored the relationship between innovation and populism and, specifically, the spatial distribution of technology creation and commercialization across the United States and how it maps onto electoral support for Trump. Nor have they evaluated whether there is a historic connection between areas that supported Trump and those that have supported populists in the past, including politicians as varied as William Jennings Bryan and Ross Perot. To be sure, some researchers attribute Trump's appeal in the Rust Belt and similar places to nostalgia for a bygone economy based on heavy industry (Cohn 2016a). Autor, Dorn, and Hanson (2016) show that increased import-competition from China significantly decreased wages and employment in the Rust Belt and Midwest. Autor et al. (2020) find that Chinese imports induced a big rightward political shift that predated Trump's 2016 election and helps explain his surprising win that year.[9] Further, several scholars have found evidence that automation reduced wages and employment in similar ways as that associated with Chinese import competition (Autor, Dorn, and Hanson 2015). Frey, Berger, and Chen (2018) find evidence for a relationship between American locations' susceptibility to automation and support for Trumpism in 2016.[10]

---

[8] They made him competitive in 2020 (Williams 2020).

[9] To measure the exogenous variation in the China Trade Shock, these authors isolate the initial shares of employment in each location and industry multiplied by the growth of Chinese imports in eight developed countries. Later in this Element, we evaluate the relationship between localized Chinese import penetration and support for Trump in 2016 using a similar strategy to ensure our results, based on the idea that innovation deserts embraced Trump while innovation clusters rejected him, are robust to the trade exposure explanation for his political appeal vis-à-vis previous Republican presidential nominees.

[10] To measure the exogenous variation in automation at the commuting zone level, these authors both isolate the historical path dependence of industrial specialization captured by sectoral employment shares in 1980 and exploit robot penetration in ten European countries. Later in

While these findings have significantly contributed to our knowledge of the economic catalysts of populism and support for Trumpism, no scholars have yet analyzed to what extent the geography of US technology creation and commercialization explains the unique appeal of Trump's economic message. Researchers have not hitherto documented the spatial dynamics of innovation in the United States, let alone assessed the relationship between technology creation and commercialization and political support for Trump across both the 2016 and 2020 presidential elections.

As the United States has become increasingly more economically stratified into innovation clusters and innovation deserts in the wake of the digital revolution and the ascendance of AI, it is important to ask if Trump's economic populism helped win him votes in places with less innovation and cost him votes in places with more of it. This Element is the first, to our knowledge, to document the extreme inequality in US localities' contributions to the creation and commercialization of technology and thus the first to show that the United States is divided into innovation deserts dotted with oases.[11] We marshal this fact to add to our understanding of Trump's unique political appeal in some geographies historically associated with heavy, labor-intensive manufacturing, loss of blue-collar jobs to China, and automation; our thesis is not the typical one, however: it is not centered on the decline of industry, trade competition with China, or the rise of factory robots.

We also investigate the historical evolution of innovation inequality and whether it is connected to the recurring historical phenomenon of American populism. In doing so, we document several new patterns: We trace and discuss changes in innovation inequality over the long run. We outline how innovation inequality follows a U-shaped pattern over the long twentieth century. While it was relatively high at the turn of that century, federal government programs during World War II and especially the Cold War helped to appreciably reduce it via aggressive government funding and coordinating of basic science and R&D due to national security exigencies and Cold War politics. However, these efforts ran out of steam by 1970 when innovation inequality increased again and, by the turn of the twenty-first century, was supercharged by a digital economy rooted in vertically disintegrated global supply chains and network effects that reinforced existing geographic disparities. By the time Trump won the 2016 election, the US landscape was dotted with a few innovation oases, albeit relatively widely dispersed, surrounded by manifold innovation deserts.

---

the Element, we evaluate the relationship between localized automation and support for Trump in 2016 using a similar strategy to ensure our results are robust to the automation explanation for his political appeal vis-à-vis previous Republican presidential nominees.

[11] Economic clustering in general is very strong in the US. Take manufacturing: 446 out of 459 sub industries in this category are spatially concentrated (Kerr and Nanda 2013: 2).

We also make an important contribution to the study of American innovation by identifying the geographic and demographic factors that made the emergence and endurance of innovation clusters more likely. Inspired by Haber, Elis, and Horrillo (2022), we show that places with temperate climates – those with relatively low to moderate temperatures and moderate to high precipitation levels – were more likely to develop the quantity of biomass (and therefore food and energy) needed to drive innovative manufacturing facilities since the early 1800s. Likewise, places with denser populations in 1900, irrespective of their climates, were also likely to develop the innovation clusters associated with the Second Industrial Revolution, centered on electrification and the internal combustion engine, and the Third Industrial Revolution, centered on the microprocessor and the internet.[12]

To defend our causal identification strategy, we argue and show that geography and demography not only helped determine the spatial distribution of American innovation clusters since the 1800s, but these patterns endured over time. Throughout US history, innovation clusters have consistently hosted patent-intensive industries at the cutting edge of process and product innovation. Individual inventors and firms have conducted innovative manufacturing, if not pure R&D, in locations such as Bell Labs in Murray Hill, New Jersey. They still rely on advanced manufacturing and are R&D intensive, albeit sometimes with smaller workforces than in the past, due to both automation and outsourcing (Bessen 2015). These areas continue to be characterized by highly skilled laborers who hop between firms located in the same region.[13]

We find strong evidence for a causal relationship between the geographical distribution of technology creation and commercialization and Trump's electoral results in each presidential election.[14] We argue this phenomenon was

---

[12] The Second Industrial Revolution began after the Civil War, exemplified by the opening of the Pearl Street Electric Station by Thomas Edison in 1882, ushering in the era of widespread electrification. The Third Industrial Revolution began circa 1973, when the microprocessor (the programmable computer within a computer chip) was invented by Intel and, soon after, commercialized in the form of multiple electronic digital devices and services, including the personal computer, the internet, and, eventually, smartphones and the digital platform economy. We elucidate these claims ahead.

[13] Often, high-tech firms strategically relocate to these places so they can poach skilled workers from firms that are already there. In turn, this drives up wages, enticing even more skilled workers to migrate to innovative areas. Plus, a critical mass of tech start-ups encourages laborers to take jobs at new firms that may fail, knowing they can always lateral to another local firm (Casper 2007). This virtuous circle reinforces spatial clustering (see Gross and Sampat 2023). For the original take on agglomeration effects in general, see Marshall (1920). Porter (1998) and Moretti (2012) offer a more recent, general take on innovation clusters.

[14] We use several strategies to identify a causal relationship, including exploiting instrumental variables based on demography, climate, and geography that capture the exogenous variation in innovation operationalized as localities' patenting patterns, which we measure at different historical intervals.

driven by an economic agenda that either threatened the innovative firms that voters in these areas worked for and/or imperiled their locations' economic engines. Conversely, voters in relatively less innovative places were more likely to support Trump during both presidential elections.

Moreover, we explore historical instances of populists contesting presidential elections. We find a weak, albeit consistent association between innovation inequality and geographic variation in support for populism at the presidential level prior to 2016. We argue that innovation inequality is a more politically salient and divisive issue today, as there was less innovation inequality in the past, a more muted political response to whatever inequality there once was, and a different political economy of US innovation prior to 1980. It took several policies, such as reforms to domestic and international intellectual property protection (IP), to catalyze a knowledge economy centered on commercializing technology and intangible capital embodied by the rise of pharmaceuticals, biotechnology, semiconductors, software, smart phones and other personal electronics, and computers. It is only then that innovation differences really packed a political punch, allowing a political entrepreneur such as Trump to exploit them better than previous American populists.

1.1 The Political Economy of Innovation Clusters

The geography of innovation and technology commercialization is explained by the spatial mechanics through which new ideas are produced and disseminated. Innovation and commercialization of technology hinges on the geographically bounded transfer of information and know-how rooted in face-to-face interactions and knowledge networks with physical footprints (Breschi and Lissoni 2003). After all, knowledge cannot always be codified, as developing and mastering technology often depends on the hands-on demonstration of specific techniques (Menaldo 2021). Putting inventions into practice relies on learning by doing (Bessen 2015). In the United States there are strong agglomeration effects in terms of R&D, industrial production that develops and uses high tech machinery and tools, and human capital. This helps to explain the spatial concentration of US innovation, including technology creation and commercialization, and employment opportunities for both skilled and unskilled workers (Moretti 2012).

Consider a city such as Lowell, in Middlesex County, Massachusetts. During the early 1800s, it was a world-renowned hub for textile manufacturing. By the mid to late nineteenth century, it had transitioned to hosting cutting-edge firms that made machines and machine tools, as well as pharmaceuticals. During

World War I, another economic reinvention saw Lowell produce munitions and other war materials. After World War II, the computer revolution came to the city, in the form of Wang Laboratories. Middlesex County is now part of New England's much-vaunted innovation cluster known as Route 128. Accordingly, since 1930, if not before, Middlesex County's patents per capita have been in the top 10 percent of the distribution.[15]

Today's innovation clusters are rich in intangible capital: locations where R&D, patenting, and the commercialization of ideas and inventions take place. These zip codes boast high levels of trade secrets, patents, and know-how. They employ creative and nimble workers. While like Lowell, Massachusetts they may have once been manufacturing powerhouses, they are not necessarily places where American manufacturing has recently fled to China, or that house highly automated factories.

Innovation clusters are places with high concentrations of well-educated people who co-locate with high-tech firms. Firms often strategically locate in such areas to poach skilled workers from other firms and access professional networks and the tacit knowledge and expertise embedded within them. A geographically bounded network of educated individuals complements the in-situ capital, institutions, and organizations associated with innovation. They also complement each other, creating network effects. However, there are often indirect network effects by which individuals with *lower levels of education* may increase their employment opportunities, productivity, and wages as a function of the number of educated individuals who reside in a high innovation cluster (Moretti 2012). Therefore, individuals with lower levels of education who might otherwise vote for populists may abstain from doing so if they reside in an innovation cluster and benefit economically from policies that promote innovation.

Take North Carolina's Research Triangle as an example. This high-technology cluster encompasses several universities, including North Carolina, North Carolina State, and Duke. It also houses firms working in Information Technology (IT) and biotech. Leading companies in the area, some of them conducting R&D there, include Apple, Google, and Toyota. While many of the region's residents are highly educated and work in high-tech industries (e.g., as computer engineers), most provide goods and especially services (finance, law, education, consulting, but also sales, marketing, HR, etc.) derived from the presence of these colleges and firms. However, many of its residents do not

---

[15] The county's patents per capita in 1930 were 0.5 (this and all figures that follow are per 1,000 people), versus a national average of 0.2 (the 90th percentile is 0.4). Its patents per capita in 1990 were 0.7, versus a national average of 0.1 (the 90th percentile is 0.2). Its patents per capita in 2000 were 1.1, versus a national average of 0.1 (the 90th percentile is 0.3).

hold college degrees and yet do relatively well economically (see Research Triangle Park 2018).

Figure 1 is a map that adduces the electoral returns in North Carolina from the 2016 presidential election. The counties in the north-central part of the state that comprise the so-called Research Triangle (contained within the black circle) voted decidedly against Trump in 2016 and did so again in 2020, as shown in Figure 2.[16] Outside of there, he had stronger support in the Tarheel State.

It turns out that the same relationship is obtained beyond North Carolina. As this Element will show in detail, US counties that were more innovative at the turn of the twenty-first century strongly rejected Trumpism above and beyond their education levels.[17] They did so both in 2016 and in 2020. And this relationship does not only pertain to the ballot box, but also reveals itself in terms of financial contributions made to Trump's presidential campaigns.

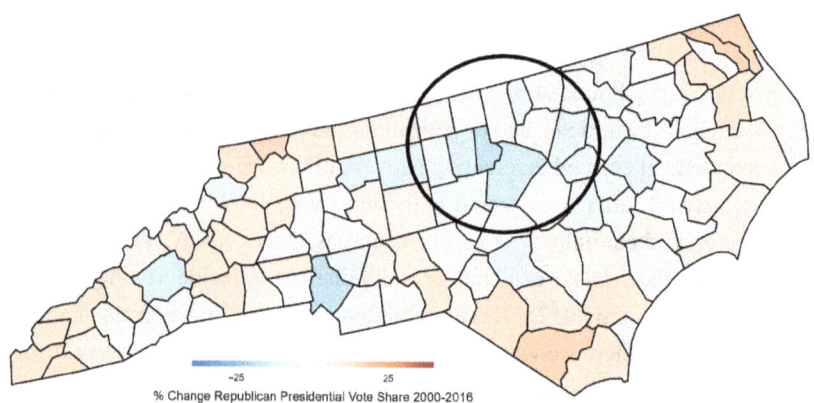

Figure 1 Electoral support for Trumpism in 2016 in North Carolina

Note: Following Autor et al. (2020), we calculate "Trumpism" by subtracting the two-party Republican vote share in 2000 from the two-party Republican vote share in 2016.
Sources: David Leip's US Elections Atlas, as used by Autor et al. (2020).

---

[16] The "North Carolina Research Triangle" is not a fixed category. Including the broadest set of research triangle counties, the difference between the two-party vote percentage earned by Trump in 2016 versus Bush in 2000 is as follows: Durham (−16.9), Chatham (−4.7), Franklin (+2.7), Granville (+2.5), Johnston (−0.8), Lee (−1.4), Person (+1.7), Vance (−6.5), Wake (−14.3), Harnett (+0.5), Moore (+1.2), Orange (−13.1), and Wilson (−7.3). The average (unweighted) difference across these counties in Republican presidential vote shares is −4.3 percentage points.

[17] In this Element, we primarily measure innovation as patents per capita and do so for several different periods, both historical and contemporary (see Section 2). We primarily measure Trumpism as Trump's 2016 presidential vote percentage versus Bush's percentage in 2000, but also compare Trump's presidential vote share to Bush's in 2004 and McCain's in 2008 and Romney's in 2012 (see Section 3).

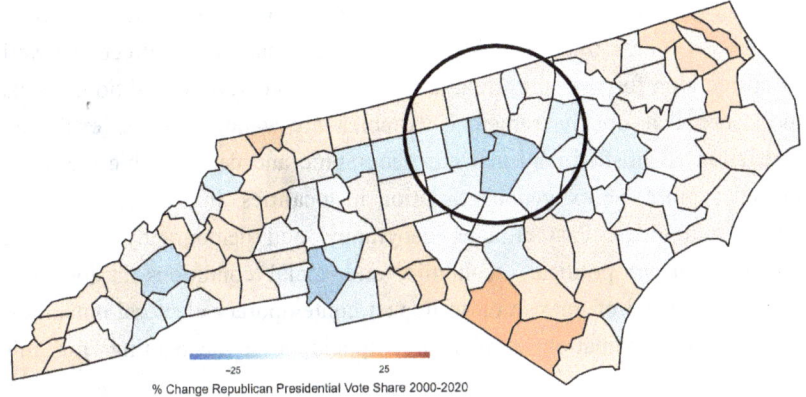

Figure 2 Electoral support for Trumpism in 2020 in North Carolina

Note: Following Autor et al. (2020), we calculate "Trumpism" by subtracting the two-party Republican vote share in 2000 from the two-party Republican vote share in 2020.
Sources: David Leip's US Elections Atlas.

1.2 Original Findings on Innovation and Populism

Our Element's main finding is that more innovative counties were significantly less supportive of Trump in both 2016 and 2020. Using both linear regressions estimated via Ordinary Least Squares (OLS) and those using different instrumental variables (IV) estimation strategies, we show that voters in innovation clusters of all sizes and across the country repudiated Trumpism in both 2016 and 2020. Moreover, we find that positive changes in patenting during Trump's presidency mapped onto less support for Trump in 2020 compared with 2016. We also show that there is a weak association between geographic innovation and support for prior populists: William Jennings Bryan and Ross Perot, respectively. We find that there is a negative relationship between innovation and support for these two populists, albeit it is weaker in both magnitude and statistical significance and, for Bryan, not robust to introducing state-fixed effects. The results of these analyses ratify the idea that Trump was different in degree from prior populists in terms of exploiting innovation inequality, but not different in kind. Why? We document relatively less innovation inequality during the Bryan and Perot eras and adduce plausible explanations for innovation inequality's reduced political salience during those periods.

Our Element's finding that more innovation equals less Trumpism is resilient. It is not driven by a location's relative demographics, educational level, economic prosperity, urbanization, manufacturing footprint, unemployment rate, and income inequality. It holds once we control for localized exposure to increased Chinese imports.[18] It is also robust to state-fixed effects, as well as corrections for spatial correlation. We also take several additional steps to ensure that our instrumental variables are valid: that the exclusion restriction is satisfied, and that our geographic and demographic measures indeed capture the exogenous variation in localities' innovation both yesterday and today. Past climate, geography, and demography may have affected current political, economic, and social conditions in localities beyond the level of innovation to impact contemporary electoral outcomes; yet our IV estimation results are upheld after accounting for this possibility.

Our main results are also unaffected by other robustness tests. They hold when using different measures of innovation: either as patents per capita in 2015, patents per capita in 2008, patents per capita in 1990, patents per capita in 1930, or the change in the stock of patents between 2016 and 2020. They are robust to whether we relegate attention to counties outside of three prominent innovation clusters: Silicon Valley, Route 128 in New England, and the North Carolina Research Triangle. Finally, our results are also robust to capturing the geographic variation in support for Trump differently: measured as his county level campaign contributions.

1.3 Bidenism as Trumpism 2.0

In the 2020 election, President Biden was forced to significantly change course on the economic policy orthodoxy pursued by the Democratic Party at least since President Bill Clinton. Biden was trying to thread the needle: to win in 2020, he had to, on the one hand, appeal to his pro-innovation base while, on the other hand, peel voters away from Trump in battleground states rife with counties that have relatively low levels of innovation (Judis and Teixeira 2023). Biden did this by promising vigorous industrial policies that could revitalize manufacturing while advancing ideas aimed at more broadly dispersing the fruits of more recent innovations around semiconductors and green energy (Ruffini 2023).

Like Hillary Clinton and previous Democrats before him, Biden's political coalition depends on the residents of high technology sectors since his donors are members of this community and many of his base voters are both highly skilled workers and less skilled workers employed in these sectors. However, to

---

[18] As well as instrumenting those shocks with shift-share exogenous variables, as Autor et al. (2020) do.

win in 2020, Biden had to nonetheless remain competitive in key swing states that Trump won, most importantly the "Blue Wall states" of Pennsylvania, Wisconsin, and Michigan (Judis and Teixeira 2023). Specifically, Biden hoped to flip several counties that Trump won in those battleground states in 2016. Many were relatively less innovative than those that have become staunchly Democratic over the past few election cycles, especially on the coasts. This meant mimicking a lot of Trump's anti-innovation populism while promising to spread the fruits of innovation more broadly. Therefore, Biden's continuation of many Trumpist economic policies, including around high-tech sectors, was partly motivated by his need to regain popularity with working class voters outside of innovation hubs (Judis and Teixeira 2023).

Indeed, Biden succeeded in flipping several relatively low-innovation counties that had given Trump the majority of votes in 2016. Consider Sauk County, Wisconsin. Its patents per capita in 2015 were 0.142 per 1,000 people, considerably less than the average that year (0.168 per 1,000 people). Or consider Muskegon County, Michigan: its patents per capita in 2015 were only 0.087 per 1,000 people. Finally, consider Luzerne County, Pennsylvania, with patents per capita in 2015 that were 0.094 per 1,000 people.

To help him win those counties over, President Biden largely followed in Trump's protectionist footsteps by focusing on reshoring American manufacturing and making supply chains more resilient and less centered on China (see White House 2021). Take his passage of restrictions on exports of high-end semiconductors to China; the Inflation Reduction Act (IRA), which includes several content requirements, prescribing the purchase of US-produced batteries for electric vehicles and the domestic sourcing of minerals for these batteries; and generous subsidies for US chip manufacturing contained in the CHIPS Act. And Biden retained many Trump-era tariffs on Chinese imports, which total more than $350 billion, as well as several imposed by his predecessor on EU and UK steel and aluminum imports, among other products, justifying them on national security grounds (see Blinken 2021; Swanson 2021). Biden also added new tariffs on China, including a 100% tax on electric car imports and similar tariffs on advanced batteries, solar cells, steel, aluminum, and medical equipment.

Second, his administration imposed crushing sanctions against China's high-end technology industries, including cutting China off from AI chips designed by US firms, as well as the software and equipment used to make chips; restricted American FDI bound for China; and imposed limits on the ability of Chinese tech platforms to collect data from US consumers. Meanwhile, the CHIPS Act heavily subsidizes US semiconductor manufacturing and attempts to increase American self-reliance around fabricating both low-end and high-end chips, including granting generous tax credits for domestic chip manufacturing and chip making equipment, and awarding billions of dollars toward semiconductor R&D.

Third, the (IRA) subsidizes US clean energy and electric vehicles and their charging infrastructure. It promotes investments in minerals, green energy manufacturing, batteries, renewable energy production, energy efficiency, hydrogen, biofuels, and carbon capture. It also awards tax credits for locally manufactured battery cells and modules; contains content requirement prescriptions, namely, "Buy American" or "Buy North American" clauses for both raw materials and inputs; compels employers to hire workers trained via registered apprentice programs run by unions; and prescribes union scale wages for firms receiving subsidies.

Finally, President Biden also promoted multilateral coordination around more managed trade within trade blocs instead of investing in new multilateral trade agreements centered solely on freer trade, capital flows, and IP protections. An example is the Indo Pacific Economic Framework, which contains tax and subsidy arrangements, anti-corruption measures, technology standard setting aspirations, coordination between members' industrial strategies, efforts to reduce carbon emissions via green industrial policy, and efforts to offset China's Belt and Road Initiative with hundreds of billions of dollars for energy, physical, and digital infrastructure initiatives.[19]

These policies directly benefited several counties in Rust Belt states. For example, consider public investments that approximate $10 billion to Wisconsin's manufacturing sector and infrastructure development, including spending on transportation, sanitation, and broadband delivery (White House 2023). The Biden administration also promoted workforce development and training across the Badger State, as well as provided financial support for small businesses and employment (White House 2023). Moreover, the CHIPS Act subsidized the construction of an Intel chip plant in Columbus, Ohio, and several new Micron chip plants, including in upstate New York and Boise, Idaho. And, incentivized by the (IRA), Honda, GM, and other car companies poured billions of dollars into the Midwest to build new Electric Vehicle and battery plants. Hence, the Biden Administration bucked a neoliberal consensus that eschewed overt industrial policy; while it was first overturned by Trump, it was consolidated by his successor (The Economist 2023).

This political dynamic is broadly in line with earlier instances of electoral challenges by populists in American political history, in which electoral demands first advanced by radical outsiders, such as Bryan and Perot, are co-opted by one

---

[19] President Biden also spoke in favor of bolstering internet privacy protections, especially for children, strengthening antitrust enforcement around digital platforms' potential monopolization practices, and reforming Section 230 of the Communications Decency Act.

or both of the two major parties over time (see Judis 2016; Kazin 1998). In doing so, Biden has attempted to reverse several decades of Democrats' eroding support in the Rust Belt and similar places where voters were once employed in "smokestack industries" (Judis and Teixeira 2023; Ruffini 2023; Short 2022).

This electoral reversal of fortune began around Carter's presidency, when Democrats began to eschew Keynesian economics and an unwavering support for unions, full employment, and redistribution. Instead, Carter spearheaded the deregulation of different industries, including transportation; strengthened IP rights; and consolidated a consumer welfare orientation to antitrust policy centered on merger and anti-monopolization policies that were primarily focused on reducing prices and stimulating innovation, instead of using earlier yardsticks for antitrust actions, such as firms' size or the displacement of small businesses. Both Carter and his Democratic successors turned to public policies that were more Schumpeterian in nature, a shift within the Democratic Party associated with faction of the "Atari Democrats" who were more much more open toward globalization and saw emerging high-tech industries as the future of the American economy (Greene 2021; O'Mara 2020; Short 2022).

Consider the Clintons. President Bill Clinton strengthened free trade and IP rights with NAFTA and TRIPS, codified during the GATT's Uruguay Round in 1994, and adopted policies that strengthened venture capital and laid the foundations for digital platforms by supporting Section 230 of the Communications Decency Act, among other pro-internet commerce policies (Kosseff 2019). During her 2016 presidential campaign, Hillary Clinton published a policy proposal specifically targeted at bolstering technology and innovation (Downes 2016). She reiterated her ambition to invest in education and federal R&D, promised to issue green cards for international students who obtain graduate degrees in science and engineering, and planned to invest heavily in digital infrastructure, with a specific view toward 5G and the IOT. Clinton vowed to expand high-speed internet coverage, both at home and abroad. She vowed to improve the international enforcement of IP and facilitate US IP exports (Clinton 2015).

Departing from his democratic predecessors, however, President Biden forcefully sought to even the innovation playing field between places. This follows the logic outlined by Gruber and Johnson (2019), who argue that more widely spread federal investment in R&D may improve political buy-in to federal efforts at fostering US performance in high-tech industries.

1.4 Element's Organization

The rest of this Element is organized as follows. Section 2 contextualizes the idea that Trumpism responds to innovation inequality by situating the Element in the emerging literature on the political economy of twenty-first-century populism. Section 3 defines and measures Trumpism in 2016 and explores its geography across US locations. Section 4 introduces the Element's theoretical framework. Section 5 explores the theory's mechanisms, applying them to the 2016 presidential election. Section 6 outlines the theory's chief empirical implications and sets the stage for testing them. Section 7 evaluates the causal relationship between innovation and Trumpism at the local level in 2016. Section 8 measures and discusses Trumpism in 2020, explores its geography across US locations, and evaluates the causal relationship between innovation and Trumpism at the local level in 2020. Section 9 explores the historical relationship between innovation inequality and populism. It quantitatively evaluates the relationship between innovation clusters and support for Bryan during the 1908 and 1912 presidential elections and support for Perot during the 1992 and 1996 presidential elections. Section 10 concludes by summarizing the Element's key contributions and outlines directions for future research.

2 Contextualizing Trumpism as Populism

We are not the first to explore a connection between local economic conditions and political support for former president Trump or populism in general. Most of the work in this area focuses on the impact of globalization. Specifically, it explores both differences in trade exposure within the United States and across other developed countries.[20] This section contextualizes Trumpism's relationship to innovation inequality by placing this idea in the extant literature.

Several scholars posit that local vulnerability to imports from China help explain the Trump phenomenon. Autor et al. (2020) show that the change in the county-level two-party vote share for Republican presidential candidates between 2000 and 2016 is substantially driven by the exposure of local labor markets to Chinese imports during the early 2000s, even after instrumenting this variable with a weighted average of Chinese exports to eight high-income countries.[21] As we ourselves do in this Element, they compare the 2016 GOP vote share with the 2000 vote share because in 2000 voters were largely unaffected by the so-called China

---

[20] Of course, researchers do not argue that antipathy against trade or, by extension, the desire for protectionism, is the primary reason for Trump's election in 2016 (see, for example, Broz et al. 2021). Many scholars acknowledge that it often ranks near the bottom of voters' concerns (e.g. Rho and Tomz 2017). And virtually all scholars agree that the type of populism embodied by Trump encompasses a range of positions that includes not only protectionism, but other salient issues too, including opposition to immigration, ethnocentrism, status anxiety, and racism (Mutz 2018). However, it is not clear that Trump's anti-immigrant rhetoric and similar chauvinistic appeals helped him win in 2016 (see Hill, Hopkins, and Huber 2019).

[21] Calibrated by a location's initial industry composition.

Trade Shock, which really began in earnest in 2001, when China joined the WTO (Autor et al. 2013b).[22]

Why would more trade ignite support for populism in the United States?[23] Researchers argue that, despite remaining the world's industrial powerhouse in both absolute and value-added terms, in the face of rising imports from China and elsewhere the United States witnessed a major reallocation from manufacturing to service jobs during the 2000s (Dinlersoz and Wolf 2018).[24] This created clear economic losers.

The numbers are staggering. Acemoglu et al. (2016) estimate that increased import competition associated with China's accession to the WTO led to the loss of between 2.0 and 2.4 million jobs in US manufacturing sectors by 2011. Autor, Dorn, and Hanson (2013a) note these effects are geographically concentrated in the Rust Belt. Autor, Dorn, and Hanson (2016) add that labor market adjustments to trade shocks have been exceptionally slow in the last decade. Autor et al. (2014) show that American workers who once worked in manufacturing activities exposed to various import waves make less money, are more likely to request public disability, have higher rates of labor market turnover, and are less likely to continue to work in industrial sectors. Freund and Sidhu (2017) find that, between 2006 and 2014, American firms across industries were subject to increased competition from Chinese firms that stole their market share or even induced bankruptcy. This, in turn, damaged public finances and reduced the provision of public goods and social insurance (Feler and Senses 2017).

Researchers then connect these adverse economic dynamics with support for rightwing populism. Broz et al. (2021) show that support for Trump was higher in counties with larger declines in manufacturing employment. Autor et al.

---

[22] Che et al. (2016) qualify this finding. They show that voters in areas more exposed to trade liberalization with China at first shifted their support toward Democrats, but this reaction wanes after 2010.

[23] The relationship between greater import penetration and support for rightwing populism seems to extend beyond the United States. Focusing on Germany, Dippel et al. (2022) find that rising imports from developing countries between 1987 and 2009 increase electoral support for nationalist parties, especially for the rightwing, populist party Alternative for Germany, and especially among low-skilled manufacturing workers (see Bromhead, Eichengreen, and O'Rourke 2013 for a historical take vis-à-vis Germany). Analogously, Colantone and Stanig (2018a) show that exposure to Chinese imports increased the Brexit vote share in the U.K. In a separate manuscript, the authors show that increased import competition in fifteen Western European countries raises the regional vote share of nationalist and isolationist parties (Colantone and Stanig 2018b).

[24] US manufacturing industries are larger and more valuable than ever, but often require fewer workers due to labor-replacing technologies that have driven productivity gains (see Bessen 2015). Indeed, while offshoring has certainly contributed to some job losses in these sectors (see the works cited earlier), Acemoglu et al. (2016) argue these have been primarily engendered by rapid technological change. Whether workers in those sectors – or even politicians – are aware of these "contextualizing" facts is an altogether different story.

(2020) find that adverse economic impacts related to Chinese imports induced a big rightward political shift in general in places with majority-white populations that predated Trump's election.[25] Baccini and Weymouth (2021) document that white voters in locations adversely affected by imports, and who suffered job losses in manufacturing sectors, were responsive to Republican candidates who promised to mitigate their economic hardship. Ritchie and You (2021) show that redistributive policies targeted by Democratic politicians to voters exposed to import competition reduced support for Trump and his protectionism during the 2016 presidential race.

Further, several scholars argue that automation has also contributed to the rise of Trumpism. There is strong evidence that, like the effects of Chinese import competition, US workers in routine jobs and industries at risk of automation have suffered declines in wages and job losses (Autor, Dorn, and Hanson 2019; Dorn and Hanson 2013b; Goos, Manning, and Salomons 2014). Unsurprisingly, exposure to robots increases voters' favorability toward redistribution (Thewissen and Rueda 2019). Frey, Berger, and Chen (2018) find that locations' degree of automation, which they instrument with automation exposure in European countries, helps explain Trump's vote share in the 2016 elections. Petrova et al. (2024) ratify these findings using a similar approach and also discover that low-skilled workers who have experienced the largest deterioration in their expected lifetime earnings due to automation were the most likely to vote for Trump in 2016.[26]

2.1 Bringing Innovation into the Study of Twenty-First-Century American Populism

In this Element, we build on the idea that the protectionist and redistributive economic policies advanced by populists react to voters' resentment about trade and automation, thus earning them electoral support. Trump did not only tout protectionism when he promised during the 2016 presidential elections that he would "make America great again." Rather, import tariffs and industrial policy geared toward subsidizing American manufacturing and related industries, such as fossil fuel production, were part of a larger package of ideas based on

---

[25] See Choi et al. (2021) for similar evidence of this phenomenon after passage of the North American Free Trade Agreement (NAFTA).

[26] As in the case of trade, the relationship between greater automation and support for rightwing populism seems to extend beyond the United States. Anelli, Colantone, and Stanig (2019) focus on regions within several European countries between 1993 and 2016 and find that places with industries more exposed to robots experience increased support for far-right nationalist parties. Im et al. (2019) uncover similar findings, also within Europe, using survey data; moreover, they discover that the relationship between the risk of automation and support for extreme right-wing parties is stronger for individuals who report relatively low levels of income security.

economic nostalgia and industrial renewal. The overall message was that the federal government would help revitalize a bygone economy based on natural resources and heavy industry and centered on products manufactured in the United States, rather than look forward, toward newly dynamic sectors. In other words, by ignoring or actively opposing dynamic sectors of the American economy, Candidate Trump's message was broadly anti-innovation, or at the very least ignored more dynamic industries.

Several studies have found a convincing link between either trade or automation and reductions in pay and job losses for unskilled workers who engage in routine tasks. Some have also identified a connection between exposure to trade shocks or robots and support for Trump in 2016 and have argued that the mechanism linking these variables are reductions in income and job losses. However, scholars have yet to scrutinize the fact that innovation and the creation and commercialization of technology, which is an altogether different phenomenon from outsourcing or robotization, are heavily geographically concentrated.

Recent economic dynamism, growth, and job creation in the United States has been concentrated in urban clusters that feature high-tech firms. Ninety percent of employment growth in the most innovative US sectors – composed of thirteen of the "highest-tech," highest R&D" advanced industries – between 2005 and 2017 was concentrated in just five cities: Boston, San Francisco, San Diego, Seattle, and San Jose (Atkinson, Muro, and Whiton 2019). Highly educated workers have flocked to these cities and greater metro regions to work in internationally oriented companies producing high value-added goods and services (Iversen and Soskice 2020). These firms operate in industries centered on the design, testing, and marketing of computer hardware and software, as well as operating digital platforms, or they provide consulting, financial and legal services, insurance, and entertainment (Boix 2019).

These facts have sometimes been married to a cultural explanation that tries to make sense of a palpable political and social sorting phenomenon that may help explain Trumpism. Some scholars have argued that more rural and less educated voters have been increasingly left behind, both technologically and economically (Rodden 2019; Williams 2017). And rather than express their resentments and anxiety in a typical class-based manner, by throwing their support behind leftwing parties that advance stronger unions and increased redistribution, voters have turned against "establishment" politicians across the political spectrum (Cramer 2016).

Perhaps surprisingly, internet platforms, cloud computing providers, data centers, and software makers have fanned out across the United States and established a presence in the country's interior. Moreover, innovation in so-called hardtech continues apace, as does employment, in industrial activities involving transportation equipment, aerospace, chemicals, electronic machinery, medical equipment, and telecommunications. Manufacturing in these sectors takes place largely outside of the most famous US innovation clusters such as Silicon Valley. Indeed, several places outside of coastal regions boast specialized, highly productive plants and distribution centers and highly skilled workforces.

Many of these locations were once home to America's most innovative industries; some are new to advanced manufacturing. Both rely on process and product innovation around robotics and AI, green energy, electric vehicles, batteries, semiconductors, machinery and equipment, and biosciences. First, consider Ohio and its major metro areas. Cities such as Akron and Cleveland once produced radios, tires, and machinery, and are now known for vehicles and robots. And, after Intel finishes its planned, $20 billion semiconductor plant, Columbus might soon be known for microchips. Another example is Milwaukee, still known for machinery, tools, and instruments. Still other enduring industrial hubs that remain innovative include cities in Pennsylvania, Michigan, Indiana, Illinois, upstate New York, Minnesota, Birmingham, Alabama, St. Louis, Missouri, and Memphis, Tennessee. Nascent innovation clusters include Boise, Idaho, Provo, Utah, Des Moines, Iowa, several Sunbelt cities, Jackson Hole, Wyoming, Bozeman, Montana, Austin, Texas, Greenville, South Carolina, and Fort Myers, Florida.

Does a more systematic assessment corroborate the view that innovation clusters are relatively geographically prevalent? To find out, we henceforth operationalize innovation as patents granted by the USPTO to inventors. Patents are temporary property rights to ideas (granted for a twenty-year term that can sometimes be extended) and represent a valid, widely used, proxy for innovation.[27] Patents granted to inventors in a given location strongly correlate spatially with other measures of innovation, such as R&D spending (Acs, Anselin, and Varga 2002), and identify technologies developed by both

---

[27] A US patent application must describe a useful, novel, and nonobvious invention in great detail and, in doing so, outline a series of explicit claims that comprise the invention. Visual diagrams must explicate the claims and the patent must cite the prior art it builds upon. A professional examiner must then screen, evaluate, and approve the application and decide whether the patent should be granted or rejected. Utility patents last for twenty years and are granted for processes, products, machines, combinations of materials, and improvements upon previous patents. This includes software patents, which can be obtained in the US without affiliated hardware. Patents are also granted for plants and modifications of plants. Patents are widely disclosed in the US (easily findable through a USPTO search engine) and strongly enforced, with broad protection under the "Doctrine of Equivalents" overseen by a specialized court – the US Court of Appeals for the Federal Circuit; IP holders who sue for infringement may gain injunctive relief and, if they win, earn treble damages.

individuals and firms.[28] Thus, several researchers have used patents to operationalize innovation at the US county level (Acemoglu, Moscana, and Robinson 2016; Gross and Sampat 2020; Hean and Partridge 2021; Xu, Watts, and Reed 2019).

Figure 3 exhibits the spatial variation in patents per capita in 2000.[29] Coastal regions tend to have relatively high levels of patents per capita.[30] This is

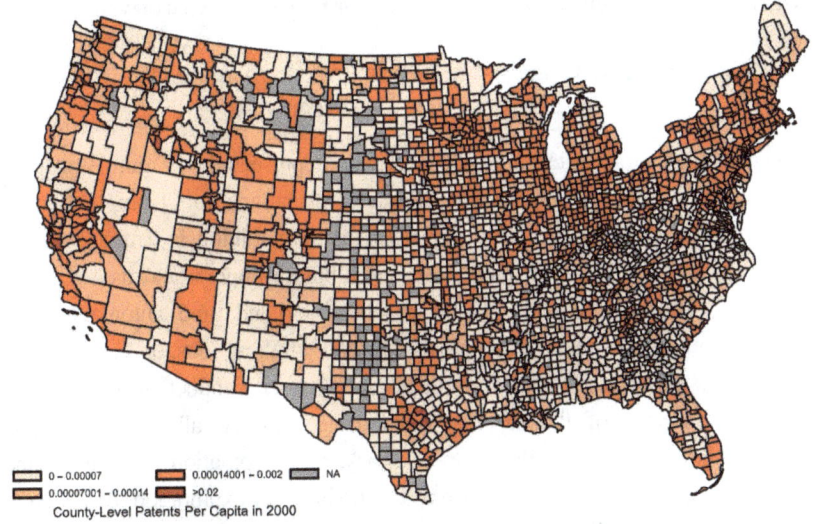

Figure 3 County-level patents per capita granted to inventors, 2000

Notes: Number of utility patents awarded in 2000 assigned to the county they originate from as determined by the residence of the first-named inventor (as appearing in the granted patent document issues by the United States Patent and Trademark Office (USPTO)). We exclude patents granted in Alaska and Hawaii to match the coverage on the Trumpism variable in Figure 6 (Section 3). We divide granted patents by the county population estimates from the US Census for 2000. NAs refer to counties for which the USPTO does not report patent data between 2000 and 2015.

Source: USPTO Patent Technology Monitoring Team (2022); US Census (2000).

---

[28] Patents are not perfect measures of innovation, however. First, not all innovations are patented. Some are held as trade secrets or are common pool resources (open source). Second, not all patented inventions are commercialized or, even if commercialized, equally innovative. Indeed, only some patents introduce disruptive innovations that introduce a whole new product line or make a big impact on an extant product's quality adjusted price; or, similarly, only some patents constitute important process inventions. Most patents represent merely incremental inventions.

[29] We follow Autor et al. (2020) and primarily use observations from the year 2000 for our independent variables to avoid post-treatment bias, including patents per capita and our controls, across both the descriptive analyses conducted here and statistical analyses pursued in Sections 7 and 8; however, we also show ahead that our results are robust to using other years.

[30] Focusing on the counties for which we have observations on Trumpism (see Figure 6 in Section 3), the mean number of patents per 1,000 residents is 0.14 and the standard deviation is 0.26.

especially the case for California and Washington State in the West and for New England and the tristate area in the East (York, New Jersey, and Connecticut). However, innovative clusters seem to be sprinkled throughout the United States. They are also readily apparent in Florida, Colorado, New Mexico, the Southwest, Texas, and the Midwestern states, especially the Great Lakes region. Figure 3 suggests that the creation and commercialization of new technologies is distributed quite unequally, however, as some areas are innovation deserts and evince very low levels of patents per capita or no patents whatsoever.[31]

2.2 Innovation Inequality Feeds Populism Separate from Globalization and Automation

How does the pattern of technological inequality represented by Figure 3 relate to what are the most predominant economic explanations for Trumpism? This Element provides an economic explanation for the variation in Trump's appeal that is empirically distinct from exposure to Chinese imports and its associated job losses and downward mobility, on the one hand, and automation that threatens routine jobs and the income associated with those jobs, on the other. We explore this question systematically in Section 7 when conducting more formal statistical analyses of the separate relationship between all three economic factors – innovation, the Chinese trade shock, and automation exposure – and electoral support for Trump. Next, we offer a preliminary exploration of this issue.

Figure 4, a scatterplot of county-level patenting in 2000 and counties' changes in exposure to Chinese imports between 2000 and 2008, conveys the idea that the US locations that innovate the most are not necessarily those that have experienced less exposure to Chinese trade. A scatterplot of the relationship between these variables instead resembles a cloud. While a simple bivariate regression that corresponds to the observations in the scatterplot graphed in Figure 4 yields a coefficient of 15.594, the t-statistic associated with it is 0.34 (p-value = 0.74), and the r-squared is 0. A county's innovation intensity – its production and commercialization of technology – appears to be unrelated to its Chinese import exposure.

Figure 5 shows a scatterplot of the relationship between patents per capita at the county level in 2000 and the change in exposure to robots between 2004 and 2010. The graph conveys the idea that US locations that innovate are not necessarily those that have had greater exposure to industrial robots or automation, as the relationship

---

[31] We note that there are 189 counties missing Per Capita Patents observations compared to the data coverage for Trumpism (6% of observations), which we map in Section 3, in Figure 6. Texas accounts for a relatively large number: we lack data on this variable for 40 Texan counties. We note, however, that the results reported in Sections 7 and 8 hold if we omit Texas from the analyses or if we interpolate the missing values in different ways, including coding them as 0s. Moreover, the mean and median for Trumpism is essentially the same across both the uncensored sample and the sample for which we are not missing patent observations.

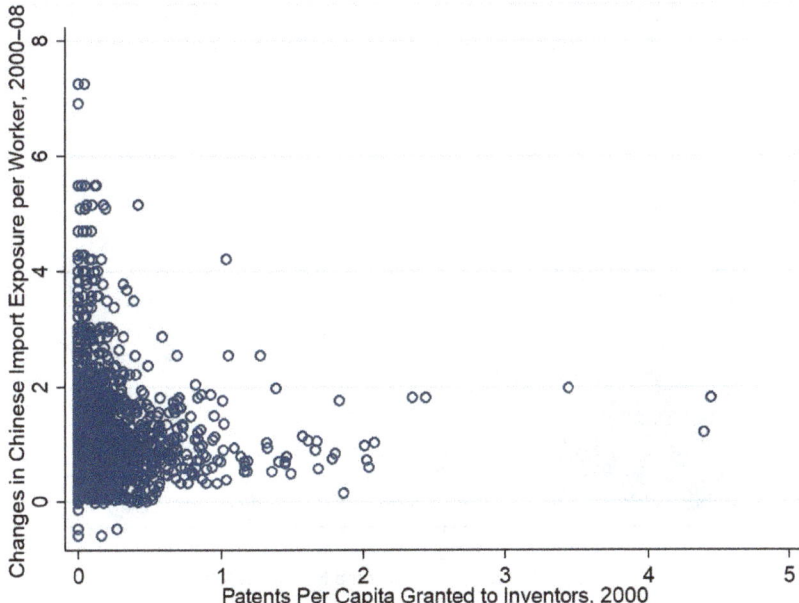

Figure 4 Innovation and Chinese import exposure in US counties

Notes: Number of utility patents awarded in 2000 assigned to the county they originate from as determined by the residence of the first-named inventor (as appearing in the granted patent document issues by the USPTO). We divide granted patents by the county population estimates from the US Census. The per capita values are expressed per 1,000 residents. The county-level changes in Chinese import exposure per worker between 2000 and 2008 capture the change in ad valorem US imports from China within a given locality (according to industries' local share of national employment) in real dollars divided by the number of workers in each location.
Sources: USPTO Patent Technology Monitoring Team (2022); US Census (2000); Autor et al. (2020).

appears relatively weak. A simple bivariate regression that corresponds to the observations in the scatterplot graphed in Figure 5 reveals that a 1 standard deviation change in patents per capita is associated with merely a 0.068 standard deviation change in the exposure to industrial robots. While the t-statistic associated with the coefficient is 2.79 (p-value = 0.005), the r-squared is only 0.005. In short, a place's innovation output, namely its production and commercialization of technology, is only weakly related to its exposure to automation.

We have now set the stage to understand how spatial patterns of innovation map onto electoral support for Trump separate from any effect made by either exposure to trade with China or automation risk. In the next section, we explore the geography of Trumpism in 2016 as a first step in understanding how it differs

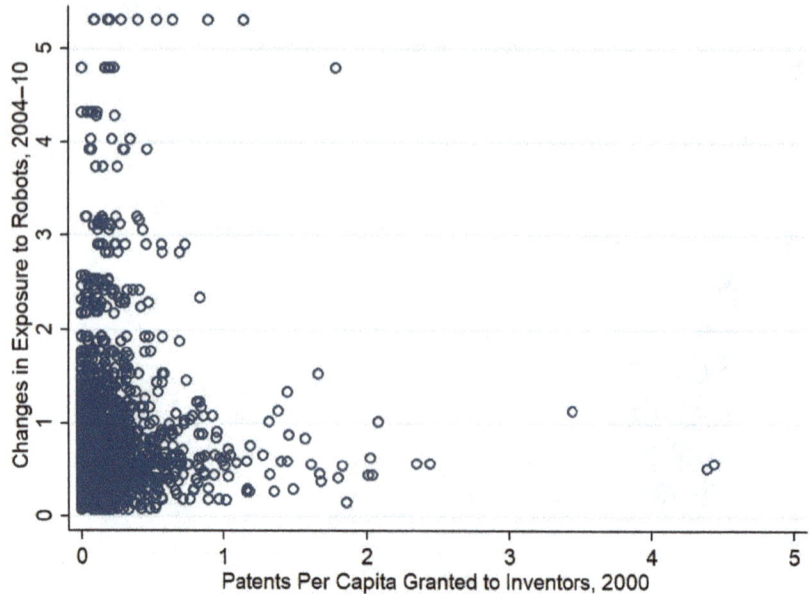

Figure 5 Innovation and exposure to robots in US counties

Notes: Number of utility patents awarded in 2000 assigned to the county they originate from as determined by the residence of the first-named inventor (as appearing in the granted patent document issues by the USPTO). We divide granted patents by the county population estimates from the US Census. The per capita values are expressed per 1,000 residents. The county-level increase in exposure to automation between 2004 and 2010 captures the average change in the local industry-level penetration of industrial robots between 2004 and 2010, based on the share of national employment according to 1990 Community Business Pattern industry data. For this graph and later analyses, we crosswalk the values originally calculated at the commuting zone to the county level.
Sources: USPTO Patent Technology Monitoring Team (2022); US Census (2000); Acemoglu and Restrepo (2020).

from more traditional conservatism and how it relates to innovation. To do so, we first define Trumpism and explain our measurement strategy. This allows us to return to the map and examine its spatial distribution in 2020 in Section 8.

3 Geography of Trumpism in 2016

This section outlines how we define and measure the Element's chief outcome of interest, the unique "Trumpist" element of the 2016 Republican vote share; we also map this variable across US counties and discuss some salient geographic patterns. In Section 8, we do the same for Trumpism in the 2020 presidential contest, as well as document county-level changes in support for Trump between the 2016 and 2020 presidential elections.

3.1 Defining and Measuring Trumpism

We seek to strip out support for conservatism per se from Trump's electoral support. We therefore follow Autor et al. (2020): the change in percentage of the two-party vote obtained by Trump versus Bush in 2000 may capture the singular appeal of Donald Trump's 2016 populist message.

Counties that are firmly conservative, irrespective of who the party nominates to run in a presidential election, should not display significant changes in the two-party vote share earned by the Republican Party presidential nominee between elections. There are Republicans who always vote Republican, no matter who is at the top of the ticket, whether it be Bush, McCain, Romney, or Trump. Indeed, they may not necessarily be big fans of the former president. However, swings away from Al Gore, toward Trump (or Gary Johnson, for that matter), point to potentially independent and liberal voters who are attracted to Trump's message. Conversely, swings away from Bush, toward Hillary Clinton (or Jill Stein, for that matter), point to potentially independent and conservative voters who are disaffected with Trump.

Of course, voters who switched their vote from Republican to Democrat between 2000 and 2016, and vice-versa, are not the whole story. There is also the possibility that voters who sat out previous presidential elections – and in this case, the 2000 edition – turned out in 2016. If they voted for Trump, this may mean greater Trumpism if their votes were not offset by voters who sat out the 2016 election. Similarly, there were voters who were not old enough to vote in 2000 who may have reached voting age by 2016; and, similarly, if they voted for Trump, this may have also increased Trumpism if their votes were not offset by voters who died before casting ballots in 2016.

In short, swings in Trump's favor vis-à-vis Bush are at least partially demonstrative of the local salience of his economic promises; swings against him, conversely, partially indicate local dissatisfaction with his populist agenda.[32]

3.2 Mapping Trumpism across US Counties in 2016

Figure 6 displays the unweighted county-level change in the two-party vote share received by the Republican presidential candidate between the 2000 and 2016 elections. Locations differed substantially in their reaction to Trump. For the 3,107 counties with data, the variable's mean value is a 7.88 swing (change in percentage of the two-party vote obtained by Trump versus Bush in 2000).[33]

---

[32] Of course, these swings could also reflect a judgment about Trump's individual attributes, or be about something other than his economic message, such as his views on issues where he differed from Bush but were not necessarily more populist.

[33] The standard deviation is 10.2; the minimum value is −28.3; and the maximum value is 46.2. A histogram of the distribution of Trumpism, juxtaposed with a normal distribution (not shown), reveals that the data resembles a bell curve. This is attested to by the fact that the mean and

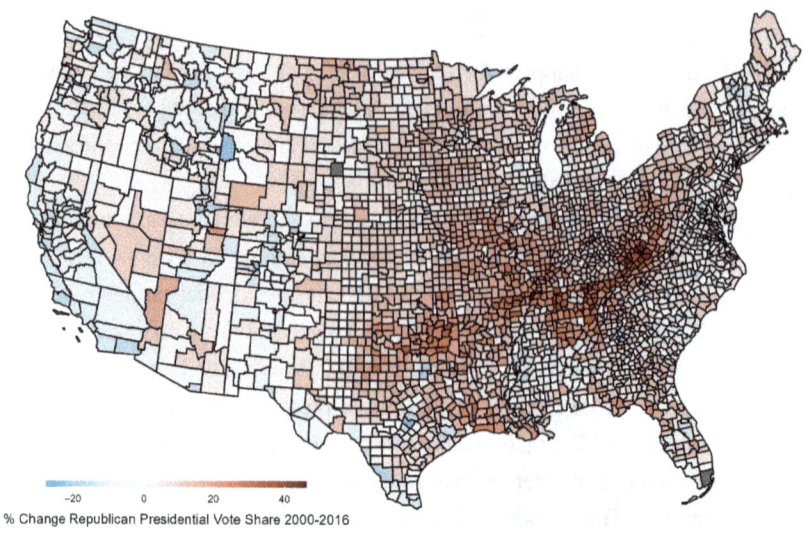

Figure 6 Electoral support for Trumpism in 2016 across the continental United States

Note: Following Autor et al. (2020), we calculate "Trumpism" by subtracting the two-party Republican vote share in 2000 from the two-party Republican vote share in 2016. Like they do, we exclude Alaska and Hawaii because of missing data.
Sources: David Leip's Atlas for US Elections, as used by Autor et al. (2020).

There is considerable heterogeneity within states in support for Trumpism. Some examples that stand out are Texas, Washington, Arizona, Florida, Colorado, Wyoming, and North Carolina.

A closer look at the data confirms the notion that Trumpism is meaningfully different from traditional support for the Republican Party.[34] Counties in red states that voted Republican in aggregate in 2016, including Texas, Florida, Arizona, and Utah, swung firmly against Trump relative to Bush. Conversely, Trump registered strong electoral gains in the Appalachian and Midwest regions, especially the Rust Belt.[35]

Why do we expect the local level of innovation to be connected to the local appeal of Donald Trump in 2016? As a first step in offering an answer, in the next section we outline a theoretical framework that connects the literature

---

median are essentially identical: 7.9 and 8.2, respectively. If we weigh this variable by the county's total votes in 2000, which we do in the regressions that follow, per Autor et al. (2020), the mean change between 2000 and 2016 is −0.74 and the standard deviation is 9.95.

[34] In Section 7, when evaluating the relationship between how innovative a county is and support for Trumpism, we show that our results are robust to comparing Trump's votes to both McCain in 2008 and Romney in 2012.

[35] Michigan, Wisconsin, Iowa, Pennsylvania, and Ohio are key states that Trump "flipped" in 2016: that is, that Romney lost in 2012.

on trade and technology to make sense of the political economy of innovation, globalization, and protectionism.

4 Theoretical Framework

In this section, we discuss why American innovative firms in innovation clusters and their workers and unskilled workers who live and work in these hubs tend to support globalization and innovation policies associated with globalization. Therefore, we explore why across education and skill levels, citizens who live and work in innovation clusters fear populist policies that promise to disrupt the global supply chains and international technology transfer relied upon by US firms operating in high-tech sectors such as software, hardware, machinery, vehicles, biotechnology, aerospace, telecommunications, diagnostics, chemicals, and green energy.

We take several steps to do so. We first examine the static and dynamic efficiency benefits of globalization generally, as well as discuss its distributional advantages for developed countries and especially the United States. We then explain why globalization's benefits are even more pronounced for US firms that specialize in intangible capital and operate in innovation clusters. We next discuss why these firms' workers, both those who are relatively skilled and unskilled, benefit from globalization and policies that explicitly promote innovation. Conversely, we explain why Americans outside of innovation clusters may not always benefit from the economic policies favored by innovative firms and their workers; they may thus be open to populist promises to reverse globalization, including curtailing immigration.

4.1 Globalization and Efficiency

By allowing nations to position themselves at the optimal location on their production possibilities frontier, international trade engenders static efficiency: specialization along the lines of comparative advantage reduces the costs of producing the goods and services exchanged between trading partners, therefore lowering their prices. When scarce raw materials, inputs, goods, services, and capital can flow across international borders with fewer impediments, they can be allocated to their more efficient use. What that means is that international market prices – exchange ratios between goods – improve economic coordination, ensuring that scarce resources are directed to where their opportunity costs are lowest and they are most valued.[36]

---

[36] Therefore, the benefits of inbound foreign direct investment (FDI) for developed countries mimics those conferred by their ability to import raw materials, inputs, and products from abroad. They can consume more foreign-made products and services and, along with portfolio investments, this allows them to run trade deficits, while also reducing interest rates on their sovereign debt. In turn, borrowing costs for private borrowers and inflation are both reduced (see Menaldo and Wittstock 2021).

International trade also engenders dynamic efficiency. By helping countries acquire new ideas, technology, and business processes from abroad, trade between countries shifts out demand and supply curves for goods and services – sometimes pushing out nations' entire production possibility frontiers in the process – and promotes increased productivity and reductions in quality adjusted prices. Coupled with international capital flows, this sometimes helps technology to flow from the developing world to the developed world (Menaldo 2021; Menaldo and Wittstock 2021).[37]

4.2 Innovative Places Have Benefited from Globalization

US firms have transformed their industrial organization to exploit twenty-first-century technology in ways that have compounded the static and dynamic efficiency gains associated with globalization.[38] Across several high-tech industries, product cycles now experience relatively high levels of turnover, making it costly for top-heavy firms that are vertically integrated to keep up with an accelerated pace of innovation. Instead, with a few exceptions, smaller and more nimble firms that are members of global innovation ecosystems occupy unique niches. Their comparative advantage tends to be tailored to only one segment of their products' supply chain: they specialize in either invention, or design, or testing, or packaging, or marketing, or retail, rather than all simultaneously.[39] Accordingly, they have honed a singular focus on intangible capital consisting of R&D, IP, and a highly skilled workforce.

American high-tech firms specializing in the design and commercialization of processes, products, and services benefit from reducing costs or introducing new products that consumers are willing to pay a premium for. Globalization helps American firms that specialize in higher value-added endeavors in vertically disintegrated global supply chains to reach economies of scale, both on the supply and demand side (i.e., network effects), reduce costs, and innovate consistently. Also, freer trade creates new export markets for the goods and services offered by these firms.

---

[37] The US is a big recipient of FDI from China, India, and even Mexico. Indeed, billions of Mexican pesos flow yearly into businesses located in the United States that make food and beverages, auto components, plastics, and provide services. While this creates American jobs and helps reduce consumer prices, it also introduces the United States to Mexican technology and knowhow. Consider the flow of technology from Japan to the United States after World War II, including both product (e.g., electronics and cars) and process (e.g., robots and steelmaking) innovations.

[38] Almost 30% of world trade takes place within firms that import both inputs and goods manufactured by their multinationals' foreign subsidiaries (see Mariotti forthcoming).

[39] In Section 9, we explore how government policies helped foster global supply chains and facilitated vertical disintegration within industries.

Consider just one example: smartphones. Past buying behavior and surveys of US consumers reveal that they are willing to pay thousands upon thousands of dollars for a smartphone but typically only pay a fraction of that price. We know that consumers bought 1G phones for $10,500 in 2017 dollars. Taking that as a lower bound estimate on their willingness to pay for 2022 smartphones, consumer surplus for this product runs into the trillions of dollars.[40] It is produced in a globally disintegrated supply chain and includes "fabless" American semiconductor companies like Qualcomm, which focuses exclusively on designing high-performance chips that allow smartphones to communicate with telecommunications networks. While Taiwanese firms fabricate these modem chips, Qualcomm reimports the final, finished semiconductors to market and ship them.

Relatively free international trade allows this innovative company to dedicate itself entirely to what it does cheapest (with the fewest opportunity costs): designing chips. In turn, Qualcomm reduces its costs and increases its profits, buoying its R&D budget and allowing it to continually improve its chips, which become cheaper (in quality adjusted prices) over time. Other smartphone ecosystem players including Apple, Motorola, Google, sundry app developers, and social networks such as Facebook; they similarly benefit from globalization. Consumers abroad who purchase iPhones generate jobs for American software engineers, app developers, and factory workers, including makers of complementary products such as headsets (many are manufactured in Colorado).[41] And as Apple and other high-tech firms have helped China participate in international supply chains, it has also become a top export market for nondigital US companies that also focus on innovation, including Boeing, General Motors, Coca Cola, and Nike, and their domestic suppliers too. For example, General Electric manufactures jet engines in Ohio to power Boeing 787s made in Washington State that are purchased by Chinese airlines.

Access to international supply chains and key export markets translates into higher paying jobs for skilled workers, including in manufacturing, and complementary service sector jobs, especially for workers who master the skills associated with digital technologies (Bessen 2015: 118; Goldin and Katz 2009). The benefits go beyond computer scientists and roboticists: white-collar professionals in finance,

---

[40] See Galetovic and Haber (2017) on all these points.
[41] By extension, the Taiwanese foundries that manufacture these chips pay relatively high wages to workers who may, in turn, consume not only more smartphones but other developed world goods and services too. The same goes for Chinese firms that fabricate and tests American designed chips. Despite Washington D.C.'s restrictions on American semiconductor exports to China, it is the second biggest consumer of semiconductors designed and produced by American companies (Leibovici and Dunn 2022).

law, education, sales, human resources, and marketing also experience pronounced spillover effects, as do blue-collar technicians, machinists, and facilities operators.[42]

The distribution of these benefits varies in space. Innovation clusters attract high concentrations of well-educated people who co-locate with high-tech firms in innovation clusters that are rich in intangible capital. Firms often strategically locate in places where R&D, patenting, and the commercialization of ideas and inventions already occur to poach skilled workers from other firms and access professional networks and the tacit knowledge and expertise embedded within them. A geographically bounded network of educated individuals complements the in-situ capital, institutions, and organizations associated with innovation. They also complement each other, creating network effects.

Both relatively skilled and relatively unskilled workers who work and live in innovation clusters benefit from this phenomenon. Innovation clusters feature plentiful job opportunities for individuals who are relatively unskilled in services and for blue-collar workers in construction, transportation, and facilities management.[43] There are often indirect network effects for individuals with *lower levels of education* who may enjoy greater employment opportunities and higher productivity and wages as a function of the number of more educated individuals residing and working in a high innovation cluster. Individuals with lower levels of education and skills may be members of geographically bound networks populated by more highly educated and skilled individuals. Membership in these networks may furnish both educated and less educated individuals with knowledge, whether it is codified or tacit, that is commercially valuable. And increased jobs and higher pay for those who are employed in innovative firms with a global footprint also generates "derived demand" for locally produced goods and services.[44]

It follows that innovation clusters populated by individuals of all education backgrounds benefit from economic policies that promote basic R&D and universities, favor immigration and freer trade, protect IP, and advance a more permissive antitrust regime. This policy mix undergirds the business models of the dynamic industries located in these areas. This translates into tangible policy preferences.

---

[42] However, one of the biggest problems faced by several American industries is a shortage of skilled workers, especially as craftspeople and laborers in precision manufacturing retire; indeed, this is the reason given by TSMC for why it has delayed plans to open a new chipmaking plant in Arizona. While low skilled laborers have sought to "upskill" to obtain higher paying jobs, employers face significant barriers filling these jobs, including inadequate vocational training (many of these jobs require a high school degree and technical skills), a mismatch between where these jobs are located and where unemployed workers live, chronic drug use problems (e.g., the opiate epidemic), and rampant absenteeism (see Bessen 2015).

[43] Indeed, an innovation hub's "multiplier effect" is an increase of five unskilled jobs for every skilled position created (Moretti 2012).

[44] For example, Boeing workers spend the money they earn making airplanes on purchasing homes and locally bought furniture, appliances, and services, such as haircuts and restaurant meals.

First, innovative US firms tend to support free trade, the liberalization of financial flows, and international institutions that include the WTO (Iversen and Soskice 2020; Osgood 2018). Second, their workers also generally support globalization (Baccini et al. 2022). This is especially the case when these firms provide goods and services at higher rungs of the quality ladder (Kim 2017). Third, individuals with lower levels of education who reside in an innovation cluster and benefit economically from its social networks and employment opportunities may also support globalization, given the positive spillover effects we outlined.[45]

4.3 Workers outside of Innovation Clusters May Not Always Benefit

There are potential losers from increased trade between developed countries and developing countries, however. In the short run, in a capital-rich but labor-scarce economy such as the United States, labor should do relatively worse because of freer trade. Assuming that capital is relatively mobile and abundant, classical distributional trade theory holds that free trade benefits capital holders (Stolper and Samuelson 1941). Rents earned by labor will be dissipated as the overall supply of labor increases, in that a previously scarce factor now competes with a more abundant pool of labor located abroad and producing manufactured goods imported by developed countries. Meanwhile, returns to capital should increase because capital is scarce abroad. Therefore, the income gap between these factors should widen.[46]

---

[45] While there is evidence that suggests that US locations fared relatively poorly after trade with China intensified (Autor, Dorn, and Hanson 2021), the most powerful explanation for increased inequality in the United States is skill biased technological change, not globalization: citizens with more education better exploit innovations associated with IT investments and similar technologies (Acemoglu 2009; Goldin and Katz 2009). Indeed, there is rather weak evidence that globalization explains increased asset and income inequality in developed economies, due in part to the fact that time-varying confounders such as automation have coevolved with increased trade and could instead explain the increased inequality between capital and labor observed in the developed world since the 1970s (e.g., Bergh and Nilsson 2010; Celik and Basdas 2010; O'Rourke 2002).

[46] While this may be true in static terms, it is not necessarily so dynamically. That is because the demand curve for labor may repeatedly shift outward over time, leading to an upward-sloping demand curve for labor over the long run. As a society gets richer, and as innovation intensifies, there will be increased demand for goods and services (hence, demand curves will keep shifting out) and, in turn, increased demand for the domestic labor who make these goods and services domestically will follow. In other words, employers will have an increased willingness to pay laborers – especially because innovation will make them more productive. While the scholars who model these dynamic effects focus on skilled (educated) labor to explain why the returns to college degrees have increased, even though the pool of college educated workers has also steadily increased (Acemoglu 2009; Goldin and Katz 2009), conceivably the same process may apply to unskilled labor too (see Bessen 2015). However, a word of caution is in order here: Autor, Dorn, and Hanson (2021) find that local labor markets that were more exposed to import competition from China experienced big declines in employment population ratios and personal

But a class-based framework is incomplete. Rogowski (1987) predicts that the relative scarcity of labor or capital in aggregate does not tell the whole story. If either labor or capital are tied to specific sectors and largely immobile between industries, then labor and capital will unite within their industry to oppose changes to trade policy that either foreclose foreign markets, if they benefit from exports, or increase international trade, if they benefit from tariffs on competing imports (see Viner 2016). Analyzing congressional voting records, Hiscox (2002) ratifies this idea, finding that when factor mobility is low, industry distinctions are more politically salient to preferences over trade. Scheve and Slaughter (2001) use surveys to show that individuals' trade preferences are partly determined by their concerns over asset values, which are tied to the performance of local industries.

The vertical disintegration of firms within several industries, characterized by varying degrees of separation between R&D, design, testing, assembly, packaging, marketing, and retail, has meant that relatively low skilled jobs in some industries *tied to specific places* have been outsourced to China and other countries. This includes toymaking in Ohio, Wisconsin, and Illinois, furniture in North Carolina and Virginia, and textiles in Pennsylvania and Tennessee. While innovation hubs no longer tend to be engines of manufacturing activities with a heavy industrial footprint within the United States (Schwartz 2021), relatively unskilled workers living in those locations have tended to find alternative employment opportunities (Moretti 2012). Blue-collar workers living in areas that lie outside of innovation hubs have faced a harder time doing so (see Moretti 2012). This is partially because high-end manufacturing has not replaced smokestack industrial production.

Consider the supply chain for semiconductors: extremely specialized and globalized, it is a completely vertically disintegrated process where design, fabrication, testing, assembly, and packaging are separated. Moreover, the software and machinery needed for each step in the production process is made by specialized companies, some of them located outside the United States (Miller 2022). The leading chip design firms are American, while the hegemonic manufacturer TSMC is a Taiwanese firm. The leading lithographic equipment maker is ASML, a Dutch firm. South Korean firms, meanwhile, specialize in making memory chips. Until recently, before the CHIPS Act began to subsidize several semiconductor plants in places such as Arizona, New Mexico, and upstate New York, whatever chip manufacturing remained in the United States has not typically occurred outside of innovation hubs (Ball State University 2022).

---

income per capita two decades after the 2001 trade shock, which holds even after factoring in the benefits of cheaper consumer goods.

5 Why Less Innovation Equals Support for Trumpism

This section explores the theoretical framework's mechanisms. Specifically, it outlines how during the 2016 presidential election, Candidate Trump's sometimes vague populist rhetoric concealed tangible policy proposals. They heralded winners and losers. We explore what Trump said about economic policy and promised to deliver if elected. We explain why voters in innovation clusters had strong economic incentives to reject Trump's contempt of high-tech industries and instead embraced Candidate Clinton's more innovation friendly policies. In Section 8, we document how, once elected, President Trump followed through with his innovation skepticism, contrasting his administration's policies with what Candidate Biden proposed during the 2020 elections.

5.1 What Trump Said and Promised to Deliver

In the run-up to the 2016 presidential election, Trump espoused muscular economic nationalism informed by the grievances voiced by residents of regions that were "left behind" by globalization and missed out on the prosperity associated with innovation clusters. Candidate Trump presented himself as an outsider who would "drain the swamp", reverse globalism ("build a wall" and "bring jobs back"), and faithfully represent the interests of America's "forgotten men and women" (Conley 2018; Williams 2019).

Only after much research, Candidate Trump explicitly targeted anxious working-class voters in less innovative, relatively unprosperous areas in 2016 – promising to return lost industries to past glory.[47] Many of these potential voters worked in, or were laid off from, declining manufacturing sectors such as automobiles, mining, and steel (Conley 2018). He targeted anti-globalization appeals to the Rust Belt in particular (see Davidson 2016; Pacewicz 2016).

Candidate Trump proposed several policies designed to appeal to voters living and working in places with declining industries, including those centered

---

[47] Contrary to conventional wisdom, these appeals were not based on Trump's preternatural political instincts. Nor were they impulsive. Trump and his advisors began planning his campaign strategy and policy platform as early as 2011, determining what voters to target and how (Conley 2018; Sherman 2016). While the 2009 Tea Party Movement portended a potential base composed of working-class white Americans anxious about economic and social change who lived primarily in the Midwest, it was only after intensive research that Trump targeted these voters with a precise message (Cohn 2016b; Conley 2018; Tesler 2016). Even before Trump declared his candidacy for president on June 16, 2015, Trump's election team picked a policy program, talking points, and slogans that mirrored preexisting sentiments expressed by potential voters in areas they deemed critical to his electoral coalition, including, but not restricted to, Tea Party strongholds. They crafted their messaging around detailed and data-driven research (Conley 2018). They spent at least $100,000 a week on polling, and paid $5 million to Cambridge Analytica, a data analytics firm, to create psychographic profiles of potential Trump voters (Green and Issenberg 2016; Grassegger and Krogerus 2017; Hope 2016).

on natural resource extraction and manufacturing. Like conventional Republicans, Trump promised low-touch regulation and tax-cuts. Unlike establishment conservatives, he also promised to curtail immigration, bring back blue-collar jobs via industrial policy, slap tariffs on imports, and renegotiate trade deals or bilateral trade relationships – especially with China.

Candidate Trump targeted places that specialized in mining, promising to reinvigorate the American fossil fuel energy sector. Specifically, if elected president, he vowed to approve the Keystone XL pipeline project, dramatically scale back the Environmental Protection Agency, "save the coal industry," achieve energy independence, and cancel the Paris Climate Agreement (Hejny 2018).

Candidate Trump also floated several protectionist measures that he claimed would revitalize American manufacturing and create blue-collar jobs. At an aluminum factory outside of Pittsburgh on June 28, 2016, he declared "economic independence," arguing that globalization had undermined the livelihoods of American middle-class workers, and that tariffs would restore American manufacturing (Trump 2016b).

Trade protectionism was the keystone of Trump's economic platform; during his 2016 presidential campaign, Trump repeatedly singled out China and its putative exploitation of the United States and its workers. Candidate Trump spoke directly to blue-collar workers who were potentially hurt by China's entry into the WTO in 2001 (The Economist 2017). He infamously declared that: "We can't continue to allow China to rape our country, and that's what they're doing" (referring to China's large export surplus with the United States during the 2016 presidential race).[48] In his campaign manifesto, Trump therefore pledged to "cut a better deal with China that helps American businesses and workers compete."[49] The premise was that China's cheap labor steals jobs away from American workers, allowing it to flood the US market with cheap goods.[50]

These grievances against globalization went beyond China. Candidate Trump also promised to withdraw the United States from NAFTA and walk away from the TPP.[51] In a *USA Today* op-ed in March 2016, Trump warned that the TPP was a direct threat to the US auto industry (Trump 2016a). He also threatened to slap tariffs on European imports – criticizing Germany's large trade surplus and specifically stigmatizing the preponderance of German-made cars on American streets (Jacoby 2020; Taylor and Rinke 2017).

---

[48] Diamond (2016).
[49] See, for example, BBC (2016).
[50] These grievances also included China's supposed currency manipulation and its subsidies of state-owned enterprises (Menaldo and Wittstock 2021).
[51] The TPP is a free trade pact agreed to by Australia, Brunei, Canada, Chile, Japan, Malaysia, Mexico, New Zealand, Peru, Singapore, and Vietnam.

Conversely, Trump's economic agenda may have repelled voters tied to high-tech sectors. This includes both white- and blue-collar workers employed in semiconductor and computer hardware manufacturing, e-commerce, and software and internet services, as well as in other innovative areas beyond the digital economy, such as higher education. As outlined earlier, these industries rely on international trade, both to establish and to coordinate complex global supply chains and access foreign markets that consume their exports. They also benefit from federal investments in basic science, R&D, and education. And they depend on skilled labor, which means they have a stake in a liberal immigration policy for high-skilled foreign workers.

Trump promised tariffs on specific imports and road-tested mercantilist policies during the 2016 campaign that would ostensibly benefit American workers but were certain to hurt innovative firms and their employees in the process. First, forcing US firms to hire American citizens over foreign-born workers or re-shore production to the United States (Trump 2016b).[52] Second, promoting content requirements such as compelling infrastructure projects to utilize US-made steel (Trump 2016b). Third, promising to bring antitrust lawsuits against high-tech companies.

Consider Trump's complaints against several big tech firms' market power. He accused Amazon of being a retail monopoly, even though, at the time, prices on its goods and services were falling like a stone as its costs kept declining, and it continued to plow its profits into R&D, allowing it to innovate across industries such as e-commerce, cloud computing, entertainment, and retail.

Candidate Trump threatened to curtail immigration, both illegal and legal. He promised to tighten immigration laws, remove all undocumented immigrants, cancel visas to foreign countries that did not take undocumented immigrants back, triple Immigration and Customs Enforcement personnel, amend the J-1 Visa Jobs Program, increase visa fees, limit legal immigration, cancel funding for sanctuary cities, build a wall on the southern border, and ban Muslim immigrants (Trump 2016c).

Many of these policies were slated to harm high-tech firms and their workers and communities. On his campaign website, Trump declared he would end the "abuse" of the H-1B Visa Program, which is heavily used by tech companies to recruit foreign talent (see Lee 2016). His antipathy toward the Common Core educational standards program also threatened high-tech firms, who have long argued for educational reforms that can help increase the ranks of so-called STEM (Science, Technology, Engineering, and Math) workers (see Carey 2016).

---

[52] For example, Candidate Trump hectored Apple to make iPhones in the United States (Lapowsky 2016).

5.2 Trump's Neglect of Innovation and Tech Leaders' Reactions

We hasten to emphasize that besides floating policy proposals that threatened to harm high-tech firms and other innovative industries, and unlike Candidate Clinton, Candidate Trump never explicitly discussed technology or innovation during his campaign.[53] Revealingly, he did not vow to create US jobs in semiconductor manufacturing. In fact, Trump lacked an explicit technology and innovation strategy altogether. Indeed, in the rare instances he did publicly speak about high-tech companies, Trump articulated disdain or personally attacked their leaders.

Evidence from Candidate Trump's social media feeds bear this out. Between Trump's announcement he was running for president on June 16, 2015, and the Presidential Election on November 12, 2016, Trump sent out 7,779 tweets (including retweets).[54] Whenever Trump mentioned terms such as "industry" or "manufacturing," he never referred to high-tech sectors. In fact, in one of the few tech-related tweets Trump sent during this timeframe, and the only one that mentioned "Apple" by name, he called on the company to decrypt an iPhone associated with a suspected terrorist couple from San Bernardino, California who had orchestrated a mass shooting against their coworkers.[55] Conversely, Trump's tweets about manufacturing were always about industries such as automobiles and steel, or adjacent sectors such as coal and energy.

Candidate Trump's skeptical, if not openly hostile, stance toward high-tech industries was unprecedented. There has generally been broad bipartisan support in Washington, D.C. for technology and innovation, especially after the end of World War II. If anything, Republicans had staunchly supported high-tech sectors since the Reagan administration, which granted industries such as semiconductors, hardware, software, and telecommunications generous concessions during the 1980s. This included reductions in capital gains taxes and subsidies for venture capital and R&D spending, favorable immigration policies, government procurement of high-tech products, especially related to defense spending, and improved IP enforcement (O'Mara 2020).[56]

---

[53] The one notable exception is that Candidate Trump vowed to end the alleged abuse of American IP by Chinese firms. However, many of his accusations were specious, and his proposals to improve the situation were mercantilist (see Menaldo and Wittstock 2021).

[54] To arrive at this conclusion, we searched through Trump's 7,779 tweets using a list of technology-industry related keywords. See the Trump Twitter Archive: www.thetrumparchive.com/.

[55] The tweet can be found here: www.thetrumparchive.com/?searchbox=%22iphone%22.

[56] In contrast to Candidate Trump, the Republican Party's 2016 campaign platform did make some efforts to parrot the GOP's typical commitments to US innovation: repeating Trump's concerns over China's IP infringement, it framed these as a national security issue. The platform also made some promises to create a business-friendly environment for innovative companies and gave lip service to tax policy, education, and infrastructure (Republican National Convention 2016).

Tellingly, several notable high-tech luminaries, many of them conservative, firmly opposed Candidate Trump.[57] In March 2016, the CEOs of high-tech companies including Apple, Tesla, Napster, and Google met with Senate Majority Leader Mitch McConnell and House Speaker Paul Ryan to try to prevent Trump from becoming the GOP's Presidential Nominee (Grim, Baumann, and Fuller 2016). Former Hewlett Packard CEO Meg Whitman, a Republican, openly declared she would not vote for Donald Trump, pledged to raise money for Hillary Clinton, and urged other Republicans to follow suit. Likewise, venture capitalist and former Netscape co-founder Marc Andreesen, who had supported Republican Mitt Romney in 2012, declared on Twitter in early May 2016 that he was voting for Hillary Clinton in 2016 (Ferenstein 2016).[58] In July 2016, 145 leaders from the US high-tech sector (including Qualcomm, Instacart, Facebook, Apple, and various venture capitalists) signed an open letter that explicitly declared the danger of a Trump presidency to innovation and economic growth.[59]

Tech workers seemed to generally share their bosses' antipathy toward Trump. In June of 2016, Crowdpac reported that only 52 "tech-workers" had contributed to Candidate Trump's presidential campaign, compared with 2,087 contributions for Candidate Clinton.[60] In July 2016, data from the Federal Election Commission (FEC) corroborated this picture: among high-tech companies, Google employees donated the most to Candidate Clinton, followed by workers employed by IBM, Microsoft, Amazon, and Apple; few workers at high-tech firms donated to Candidate Trump. Meanwhile, individuals employed in finance, manufacturing, and agriculture were among the top donors to his 2016 campaign (see Perlstein 2016).

Combined with our theoretical framework, this section's interrogation of Trump's economic policies generates clear predictions about the 2016 US presidential election. The next section is dedicated to outlining those, as well as spelling out other hypotheses about the history of American technological progress and innovation clusters. This will allow us to set the stage to systematically test our main empirical implications in Section 7 using

---

[57] While PayPal cofounder and famed venture capitalist Peter Thiel is a notable exception, he would not have been much of an outlier before 2016. While certainly more cosmopolitan and liberal leaning than the rest of the country in general, not all voters living in Silicon Valley, Seattle, New England's Route, and North Carolina's Research Triangle have historically been lockstep supporters of the Democratic Party; nor have the leaders of the tech firms headquartered there (see O'Mara 2020).

[58] Andreesen's original tweet has since been deleted. During the 2024 election he endorsed Trump.

[59] The letter stressed the importance of maintaining liberal immigration policies, and the government's key role in investing in infrastructure, education, and scientific research (see "Trump Would Be a Disaster for Innovation" in Stanton 2016).

[60] "Tech-workers" is a capacious category that includes Gig-workers such as Uber drivers.

a county-level dataset. In Section 8, we again test these empirical implications using not only 2020 presidential election data, but also financial contributions made to both of Trump's presidential campaigns.

6 Setting the Stage to Test the Theoretical Framework's Implications

This section outlines our theoretical framework's empirical implications. We spell out our key hypotheses; take a first look at the evidence; hash out a strategy for exploiting exogenous variation in innovation clusters as a way of causally identifying the relationship between innovation and Trumpism; and report significant path dependence in US innovation clusters since the early 1800s. In Section 7, we evaluate the empirical implications for the 2016 presidential election. In Section 8, we do so for the 2020 presidential election.

6.1 The Major Empirical Implications

In 2016, voters in US innovation clusters, however small, should have reacted negatively to Candidate Trump's calls for protectionism and his associated threats to technology transfer, global supply chains, R&D, skilled foreign workers, and the creation and commercialization of innovative products and services. His promises to disrupt the international liberal architecture, including free trade agreements and international institutions such as the WTO, threatened the innovative firms these voters worked for and the communities hosting them. Second, innovation clusters that are highly productive and only loosely connected to the global economy may have also rejected Trump's general bid to "make America great again" – or, in other words, take the US economy back to a past populated by vertically integrated and fossil fuel intensive firms operating in heavy industries.

The converse should also be true. Firms that are less innovative should have responded positively to Candidate Trump. They may favor protectionism outright or be less averse to other anti-globalization policies that threaten to hurt R&D and the commercialization and diffusion of technology. These may include restrictions on the immigration of skilled workers and less government support for basic science and higher education. The same should hold true for their workers and the residents of places that host them.

In the 2020 presidential elections, the same patterns should have held true. Moreover, support for Trump in America's more innovative US counties should have experienced further erosion between the 2016 and 2018 contests, albeit this electoral softening should be relatively muted: given that he had amply revealed his economic policy platform during the 2016 presidential campaign, voters in both innovative and less innovative places should have already priced in President Trump's populist challenges to innovation clusters by the 2020 elections. Notwithstanding that fact, because Trump followed through and implemented several innovation-retarding ideas during his presidency, including some he had not yet previewed in 2016 – something we will document in Section 8 – Trump should have experienced a greater reduction in campaign contributions in 2020 versus 2016 in more innovative US counties.

6.2 A First Look at the Evidence

What is the spatial relationship between innovation and Trumpism? As a first step, we can compare the map of innovation at the US county level represented by Figure 3 in Section 2 with electoral support for Trump in 2016 (versus Bush) in Figure 6 in Section 3. Visually, it is obvious that innovative places' support for Trumpism was relatively low in 2016. As a second step, consider a bivariate linear regression estimated via OLS with counties as the unit of analysis. It reveals that increasing per capita patents by 1% maps onto a decrease in Trumpism of 1.19 percentage points (p-value < 0.001). In Section 7, Table 1, Column 1 reports that finding.[61] In the next section, we investigate whether the spatial relationship between these variables indeed runs from the relative degree of innovation to the relative electoral support for Trump. Before doing that, however, we must do some more legwork.

6.3 Moving beyond Correlations between Innovation and Politics

The simple negative correlation between innovation and Trumpism at the geographic level outlined earlier is not necessarily indicative of a causal relationship between these variables.

On the one hand, it could be that a simple linear regression estimated via OLS may *overestimate* the negative effect of innovation on the Trump vote. It could be the case that *more politically populist places are somehow inherently less innovative*. Similarly, an omitted factor may *jointly determine both relatively low patenting per capita and high support for Trumpism*. For example, highly dense cities may be both relatively more innovative and relatively more anti-Trump. Or places with more educated voters may produce more patents per capita and may have also rebuked Trump for reasons having little to do with innovation.

---

[61] We follow Autor et al. (2020) and cluster the standard errors by commuting zone and weigh the observations by counties' total votes in the 2000 presidential election.

Table 1 The determinants of Trumpism and justifying the instrumental variables

PANEL A

Dependent Variable	(1) TRUMPISM	(2a) log(Patents P.C.)	(2b) TRUMPISM	(3) log(Biomass)	(4) TRUMPISM
Estimation Strategy	OLS	IV (Stage 1)	IV (Stage 2)	OLS	IV (Stage 2)
log(Patents Per Capita)	−1.193***		−2.219***		−2.315 ***
	[0.081]		[0.647]		[0.646]
Temperature		0.071**		0.106***	
		[0.029]		[0.027]	
Precipitation		0.132***		0.119***	
		[0.465]		[0.437]	
Temperature X Precipitation		−0.003***		−0.003***	
		[0.002]		[0.001]	
Population Density 1900		0.319***		0.138***	
		[0.067]		[0.040]	
China Trade Shock					2.072***
					[0.882]
Shift Share Instrument	No	No	No	No	No
State-Fixed Effects	No	No	No	No	No
Baseline Controls	No	No	No	No	No
Additional Controls	No	No	No	No	No
Observations	2,918	2,660	2,660	2,812	2,660

PANEL B

Dependent Variable	(5) TRUMPISM	(6) TRUMPISM	(7) TRUMPISM	(8) TRUMPISM	(9) TRUMPISM
Estimation Strategy	IV (Stage 2)	IV (Stage 2)	IV (Stage 2)	IV (Stage 2)	LIML (Stage 2)
log(Patents Per Capita)	-2.384***	-6.097***	-2.177***	-2.566***	-4.798***
	[0.667]	[1.145]	[0.675]	[0.641]	[1.759]
China Trade Shock		3.485***	3.001***	1.634	1.316	1.407
	[1.185]	[1.168]	[1.267]	[1.305]	[2.060]
Shift Share Instrument	Yes	Yes	Yes	Yes	Yes
State-Fixed Effects	No	Yes	Yes	Yes	Yes
Baseline Controls	No	No	Yes	Yes	Yes
Additional Controls	No	No	No	Yes	Yes
Observations	2,660	2,660	2,660	2,653	2,653

Notes: Significant at the 0.01 level (***); significant at the 0.05 level (**); significant at the 0.10 level (*). Patents per capita are measured in 2000. Following Autor et al. (2020), we calculate "Trumpism" by subtracting the two-party Republican vote share in 2000 from the two-party Republican vote share in 2016. Like they do, we exclude Alaska and Hawaii because of missing data. We estimate, but do not report, several first-stage regression results for the IV models. We cluster the standard errors across all models by commuting zone and weigh the observations by counties' total votes in the 2000 presidential election. See text for what variables are included in both the set of Baseline Controls, which were originally collected and used by Autor et al. (2020), and the set of Additional Controls.

On the other hand, the effect of innovation on the Trump vote might be *underestimated* in regressions estimated via OLS. The reason for this is the substantial increase in federal investment in science and technology starting in World War II that continued during the Cold War. Partly by design, this helped to promote targeted innovation in areas that had hitherto been much less innovative, partially narrowing the gap with more technologically advanced places (see Gross and Sampat 2023; Wright 2020; also see Figure 15). However, these attempts by the federal government to narrow innovation inequality, while relatively successful (see Section 9), did not really create new innovation hubs per se, except for a few instances. This would make it seem that places that were not true innovation clusters would nonetheless exhibit higher numbers of patents per capita than would otherwise be expected. These places would also be more likely to have gone for Trump during the 2016 and 2020 presidential elections, yielding an *underestimate* of the true geographic association between innovation and support for Trump.

Consider that, before World War II, most federally funded R&D was carried out in small government laboratories, experimental stations, or military arsenals (National Academy of Sciences 1995). The federal government played a minor role in supporting research at American colleges and universities, mostly around farming, mining, and petroleum, which relied overwhelmingly on philanthropic endowments or funding from private companies (David and Wright 1997).

During World War II, total federal spending on R&D increased dramatically (National Academy of Sciences 1995). The federal government's chief instrument to do so was to dole out R&D contracts to both private companies and universities. Gross and Sampat (2023) recount that the Office of Scientific Research and Development (OSRD) alone awarded over 2,200 R&D contracts throughout World War II, spending around $7.4 billion in 2022 dollars. While federal R&D spending declined overall in the first years after World War II, the Soviet launch of Sputnik in 1957 reignited federal R&D efforts (National Academy of Sciences 1995; O'Mara 2020). Figure 7 graphs R&D spending as a percentage of GDP conducted by US business and the federal government between 1953 and 2021 and shows that R&D as a share of the economy almost doubled between 1953 and 1965. It was only around 1980 that private R&D funding surpassed public funding.

Moreover, World War II ushered in a major shift in how scientific research in the United States is organized, as the federal government became much more directly involved in coordinating science and technology. Washington, D.C. became a major source of funding for science, but also mobilized substantial funds to build scientific installations for government-funded research. This practice was consolidated after the war, when several governmental agencies began to coordinate public R&D across the nation. The Atomic Energy Commission obtained

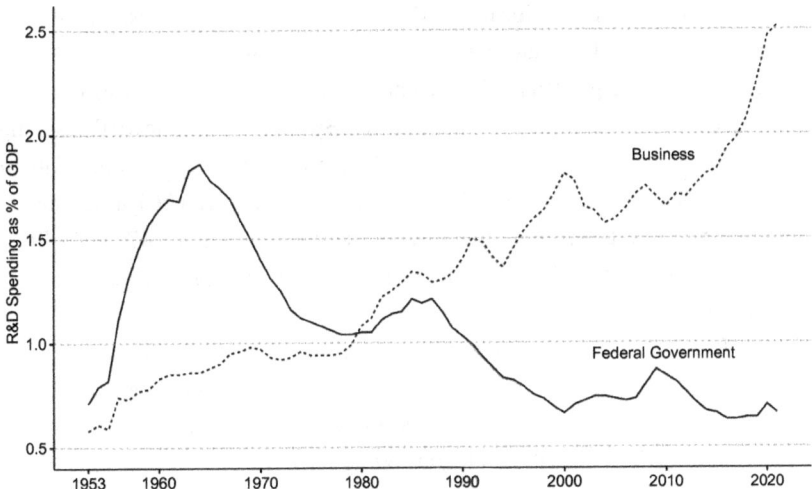

Figure 7 Public versus private R&D spending (%GDP) from 1953 to 2021
Sources: NSF; National Center for Science and Engineering Statistics, National Patterns of R&D Resources; Bureau of Economic Analysis statistics (2022).

control of nuclear weapons and choreographed R&D around nuclear power.[62] The Office of Naval Research, as well as other arms of the Department of Defense, assumed a major role in funding and supporting academic research in the physical sciences (National Academy of Sciences 1995). The National Institutes of Health established control over most health-related research, including biomedical research conducted in universities (Hurt 2015; National Academy of Sciences 1995). The National Science Foundation (NSF) was created in 1950 to directly support more basic research at US academic institutions that did not fall directly under the more mission-driven R&D conducted by other federal agencies (NSF Website).

These federal agencies began to mobilize large numbers of scientists and academic researchers in laboratories and other research installations (National Academy of Sciences 1995) that reached beyond places that had been innovative prior to World War II (Clayton 1967). These efforts created new installations and concentrated knowledge workers in areas that had hitherto been much more isolated economically and were historically innovation deserts. While Los Alamos National Laboratory, literally located in the desert, northwest of Santa Fe, is perhaps the most paradigmatic example, there are several others too.

---

[62] The mandate of the AEC, which later became the Department of Energy, has been expanded repeatedly; today it is a major funder and coordinator of most US energy-related R&D, including renewables (see Wittstock 2024).

Consider Richland, WA, located in Benton County. Today it houses the Pacific Northwest National Laboratory, part of the network of facilities funded by the Department of Energy. Richland became a site of the Manhattan Project and received continued R&D during the Cold War. By the 1950s, the town that sprang up around the governmental research installation was called the "Atomic City of the West" (see Findlay 1995: 32). While Richland experienced a substantial population influx throughout the Cold War, growing from 247 in 1940 to 33,578 in 1980 (Gerber 1992), Benton County went from producing no patents in 1940 to 42 in 1980.

Oak Ridge National Laboratory in Tennessee and other historically less innovative places were similarly showered with federal money during the Cold War. They included Albany, OR; Ames, Iowa, Aiken County, SC, Lemon, IL, Morgantown, WV, and Idaho Falls, ID. While only 185 counties were the direct recipients of over 85% of all primary military contract spending in 1960 (Isard 1962), among these counties, 9 recipients had been granted no patents at all in 1940; and 35 counties receiving substantial military contracts in 1960 had been granted fewer than 10 patents in 1950.

Further, throughout the Cold War, defense firms tended to site both R&D and some production plants close to military testing facilities dotted throughout the United States. They therefore made use of well-trained labor forces with connections to the US military (Markusen and Bloch 1985). These military testing facilities were not generally located in places that were innovative or industrial. The siting of defense-related investments was also considerably guided by considerations of regional equity and other political factors, not preexisting experience with innovative activities (Crump and Archer 1993).

Figure 8 graphs the number of counties with ten or more patents granted per year between 1920 and 2015. It clearly shows that after World War II there are several counties that are joining the innovation ranks, with many going from exhibiting zero patents to more than ten. The number of counties with 10 or more patents grew continuously between 1946 and 2000.

Meanwhile, Figure 15 in Section 9 graphs the total share of all patents granted to the top 1% of innovative counties (those with the highest number of patents per capita) by year from 1900 to 2015. It suggests that, after World War II, innovation became geographically spread around more broadly. While innovation inequality again ramped up after 1970, for several reasons we highlight in Section 9, it remains the case that Washington D.C.'s efforts to target places that were less innovative after World War II bore some fruit in raising their relative innovation output: government-funding of science, defense contracting, and the creation of governmental R&D installations created new sites of technological innovation in areas that had hitherto been innovation deserts.

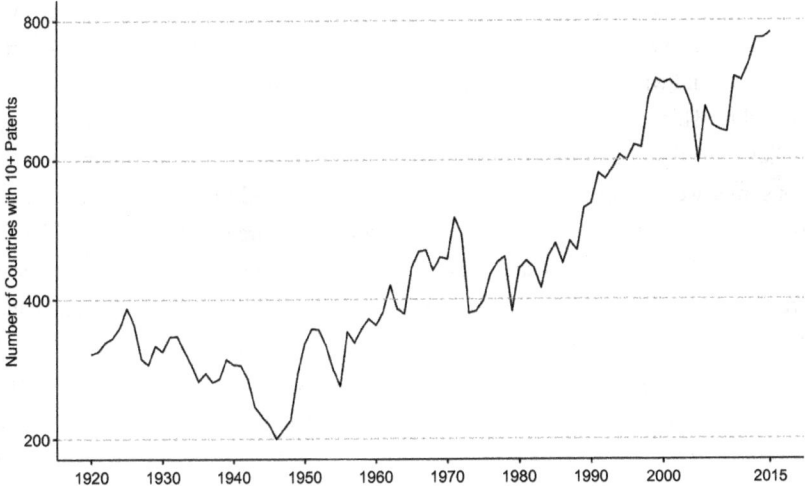

Figure 8 Number of counties with 10+ patents granted per year, 1920–2015

Notes: For each year between 1920 and 2015 we graph the total number of counties with 10 or more patents granted to inventors. We note that in 1907 Oklahoma joined the union; in 1912, New Mexico and Arizona joined; and in 1959, both Hawaii and Alaska joined. Omitting Hawaii and Alaska does not materially alter the patterns depicted in the graph.
Sources: Histpat (Petralia, Ballard, and Rigby 2016); USPTO; authors' calculations.

However, because these efforts did not necessarily translate into creating new innovation clusters akin to Silicon Valley or New England's Route 128, there is a potential discrepancy between the concept "innovation cluster", which we defined and elucidated in Section 1.1 of Section 1, and how we measure it as patents per capita, which we articulated in Section 2 (see Section 2.1). In turn, this discrepancy may create false positives that increase the noise to signal ratio: some places may seem to be very innovative (because they produce many patents due to federal efforts to even the innovation playing field), but they are not true innovation clusters in terms of satisfying the logic of spatial agglomeration and network effects. This therefore justifies an IV approach aimed at isolating the exogenous variation in geographic innovation.

Finally, there is another important reason why linear regressions estimated via OLS may be biased against finding a negative association between geographical innovation and Trumpism. Before Trump arrived on the political scene, less innovation in a particular geography may have meant more class solidarity and unionization for the workforce employed and living there and thus greater support for the typical message put forth by the Democratic Party after FDR and running through LBJ (Judis and Teixeira 2023).

As we discussed in Section 1, the Democrats transformed themselves into a more neoliberal party, first under President Carter, who deregulated large parts of the economy and was more circumspect in relation to antitrust and more supportive of IP rights. This was then consolidated under President Clinton, whose economic policy benefitted innovative firms and who championed the turn toward the consumer welfare approach in antitrust and implemented further deregulation and policies that benefited Big Tech, such as Section 230 (Greene 2021; O'Mara 2020; Short 2022). Yet, it took decades for this pivot by the Democrats to reach political fruition, as President Obama relied on support from so-called Blue Wall states in the Rust Belt that were relatively less innovative in 2008 and 2012 to gain and retain power. This political path dependence would have cut against support for Trump's populist message as it may have helped create political inertia that would have favored first Secretary of State Clinton during the 2016 elections and then President Biden during the 2020 election, despite their high-tech bona fides.

6.4 Exogenous Variation in Innovation Clusters

To establish whether there is a causal relationship between innovation and Trumpism, we exploit exogenous geographical features that made innovation more likely in certain parts of the United States during the nineteenth and early twentieth centuries. Following Haber, Elis, and Horrillo (2022), places with temperate climates – those with relatively low or moderate temperatures and relatively moderate to high precipitation levels – were more likely to develop the quantity of biomass (and therefore food and energy) needed to sustain innovative manufacturing facilities in the 1800s. In the early twentieth century, places with greater population densities, no matter their climates, attracted inventors and capitalists who commercialized new technologies, ushering in innovation clusters.

Throughout American history, efforts by firms and entrepreneurs to reduce transportation and communication costs have motivated them to strategically locate manufacturing and innovation activities such as R&D; access to relatively cheap energy has also mattered (Keer and Nanda 2013: 2). Figure 9 maps the spatial distribution of biomass (the presence of animals and plants, which proxy for crops and timber and energy: stored radiation from the sun) in the United States in 2012.[63] Contemporary biomass patterns, which proxy for historical ones, should track the location of American innovators circa 1800.

At the turn of the nineteenth century, American industrialists and innovators sought access to abundant food and fuel. For example, Haber, Elis, and Horrillo (2022: 37) recount how during this time the New York hinterland, laden with

---

[63] This variable's mean is 105,356,000 tons; its median is 69,140,000 tons.

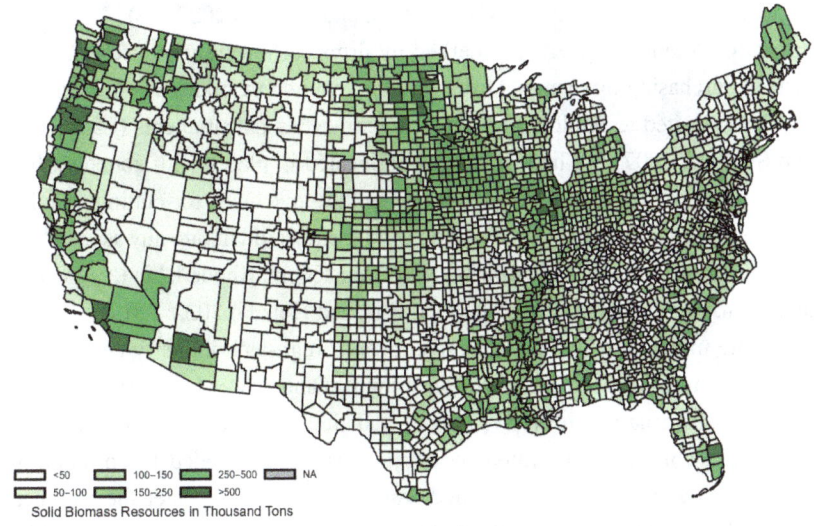

Figure 9 Total biomass resources in 2012

Notes: Solid biomass resources are measured in thousands of tons per year, including crop residues (which is the five-year average between 2003 and 2007), forest, and primary mill residues (measured in 2007), and secondary mill residues (measured in 2009), and urban wood waste (measured in 2010). This proxies for historical biomass as reliable data for biomass is not readily available before 2012.
Source: Roberts (2014).

biomass from hardwood forests and then cereal crops, attracted an agglomeration of sawmills, gristmills, manuscript mills, and manufacturers of various types. In this and other US locations like it, farmers settled and cleared forests to grow storable grains and legumes, a very salient concern for inventors and industrialists at the time: it was too expensive, if not impossible, to import food from long distances (Haber, Elis, and Horrillo 2022). In turn, this fostered accumulation, specialization, trade, finance, and manufacturing (Haber, Elis, and Horrillo 2022: 37).

Biomass also proxies for access to readily available energy sources, most obviously from burning wood but also refined crop oils. Up until the mid-nineteenth century, biomass constituted the single largest source of total annual US energy consumption (US Energy Information Administration 2022). It remained an important fuel source into the first half of the twentieth century.

The early industrialization of the US was centered on textiles, arms manufacturing, machine tools, and railroads. Several technologies were brought over from England or were developed in the United States in parallel to English and sometimes French innovations (Haber, Elis, and Horrillo 2022: 37).[64] This was the era of "the great inventor," marked by firms eschewing in-house R&D and instead purchasing innovations from serial inventors in vibrant, albeit geographically segmented technology markets, sometimes via patent agents (Lamoreaux and Sokoloff 2007).[65] These inventors collocated in places with abundant biomass, so that "[t]he invention of jigs and milling machines for cutting metal to precise tolerances, such that parts made from them would fit into any assembly of the same type, came out of workshops in Connecticut, Rhode Island, New York and Pennsylvania in the 1810s" (Haber, Elis, and Horrillo 2022: 38).

Textile manufacturing was an early form of high-tech industry centered on self-acting mules (mechanized cotton spinning) and power looms (weaving).[66] It occurred primarily in New England and the Mid-Atlantic states. Distinct innovation clusters proliferated because industrialists needed to co-locate in places with a critical mass of skilled workers who could master the technical knowledge and know-how associated with these new technologies; textile mills expended great efforts attracting literate and trainable workers, most of them women, to help run their new equipment efficiently (Bessen 2015).

What climatic conditions favor greater biomass? Soil humidity, soil and air temperature, photoperiod, solar radiation, and precipitation all impact the availability of water and soil nutrients. In turn, both are critical for fostering healthy forests and the crops that may potentially displace them (Haber, Elis, and Horrillo 2022). In the United States, abundant biomass is thus more prevalent in temperate climates with relatively high soil quality, moderate precipitation, and relatively low temperatures, as the latter reduces evaporation and plant transpiration, and winter frost helps kill parasites and pests that cause plant diseases and improves topsoil and thus soil fertility (see Khalifa 2022: 26–27). This translates into more abundant food. Plus, the cereal crops that can be grown in temperate places can be more effectively stored (Haber, Elis, and Horrillo 2022).

Figures 10 and 11 reveal the historic distribution of temperature and precipitation in the United States, respectively. Both were measured in 1900 for 2,660 counties. Temperature is the average degrees per year, with the mean and

---

[64] The authors tell how the US Patent Act of 1793 improved upon the British patent system by simplifying patent filing and IP enforcement and reducing patenting costs by 95% (see pg. 6).

[65] The federal government did not only help stimulate innovation by providing strong IP rights; it supplied a robust postal network, granted land to railroads and homesteaders, established land grant universities and subsidized agricultural and mining research, allowed liberal bank chartering that made credit widely available, spent readily on infrastructure, and conducted geological surveys that were made public. Local governments spent generously on education.

[66] Textile manufacturing also benefited from the invention of the cotton gin. And, similar to England, the United States witnessed the widespread application of new technologies beyond textiles, including coke smelting, iron puddling and rolling, and steam engines applied to mining, manufacturing, and transportation.

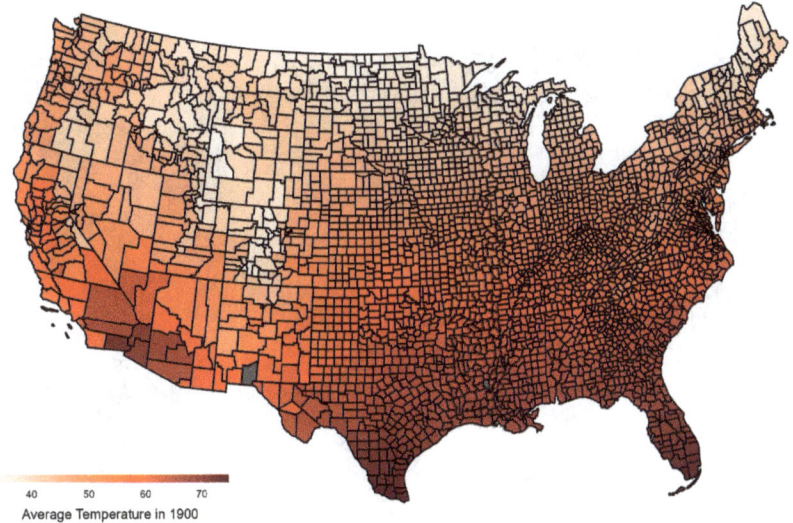

Figure 10 Annual mean temperature in 1900

Notes: Measured in Fahrenheit. The continental United States is separated into 344 separate climate divisions. For each, monthly temperature values are computed from daily observations collected from weather stations. These values are weighted by area to compute local values (Karl and Koss 1984).
Source: US Climate Divisional Database (CDD) published by the National Oceanic and Atmospheric Administration's National Centers for Environmental Information (NOAA-NCEI).

median values both equal to 53.7 Fahrenheit. Precipitation is total inches of rainfall per year, with a mean of 35.8 and a median of 37.1. These maps adduce a strong relationship between temperate climates (low to moderate temperature and moderate to high rainfall) and abundant biomass (see Figure 9).

6.5 History of American Innovation Clusters and Path Dependence

To bolster confidence in our causal identification strategy, we now explore the spatial persistence of American innovation inequality over time. The presence of abundant biomass in some US locations with temperate climates fostered early innovation clusters during the early nineteenth century. These were likely to endure and strengthen during the ensuing centuries. Consequently, the exogenous factors that explain innovation in the distant past should also map onto innovation in later periods.

Places with high quantities of food and fuel attracted innovators and industrialists. These advantages were reinforced as they drew rising levels of capital-intensive machinery, R&D activity, and talented high-skilled workers.

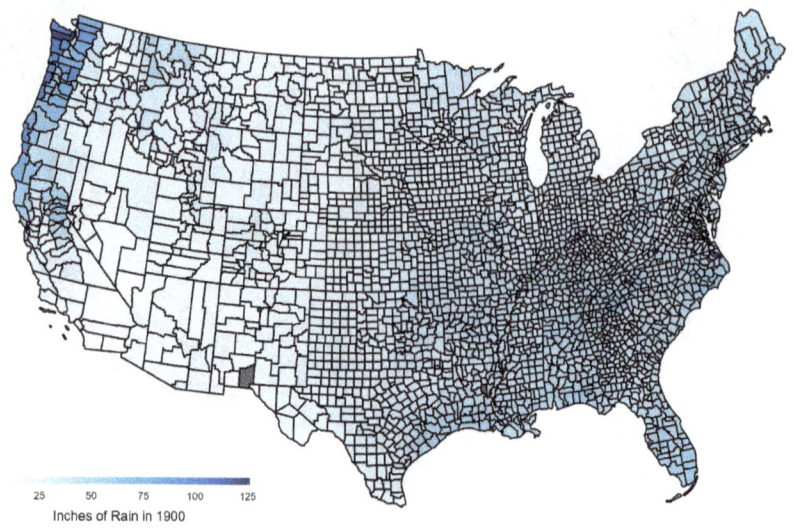

Figure 11 Annual precipitation in 1900

Notes: Measured in annual inches of rain. The continental United States is separated into 344 separate climate divisions. For each, monthly precipitation values are computed from daily observations collected from weather stations. These values are weighted by area to compute local values (Karl and Koss 1984).
Source: CDD published by NOAA-NCEI.

Geographically blessed locations were therefore more likely to continue to churn out process and product innovations over succeeding industrialization waves. And high transportation costs and transaction costs compounded by long distances limited technology transfer between temperate and nontemperate climates (Haber, Elis, and Horrillo 2022; Khalifa 2022: 28).

After the Civil War, the United States experienced the so-called Second Industrial Revolution – before any other country, and with greater intensity than its followers. This industrialization wave was centered on general-purpose technologies (GPTs) such as electricity and the internal combustion engine. During this era, there was a concomitant proliferation of innovative batch and continuous-process manufacturing. Vertically integrated, multi-divisional firms that took direct control of suppliers and distribution channels and produced at large scale emerged and reached a national, if not global, market (Lamoreaux and Sokoloff 2007). Mass-produced US exports that relied on sophisticated, capital-intensive technology exploded, and, by around 1890, the United States surpassed the United Kingdom in terms of technological prowess, industrial intensity, and overall prosperity (see Nelson and Wright 1992).

After the turn of the twentieth century, American innovation, industrialization, and productivity intensified further. Between 1909 and 1929, the United States experienced a sixfold increase in the use of electricity to power manufacturing and residential power use and a similar increase in the amount of horsepower to workers.[67] An explosion in capital-intensive process innovations around rubber, glass, petrochemicals, standardized machinery, and electrical equipment followed. New product inventions during this period included mass-produced automobiles and airplanes, radio, motion pictures, telephones, household appliances, and canned food, along with synthetic materials, dyes, and fabrics.

The Second Industrial Revolution relied on highly skilled labor. Most manufacturing jobs began to require a high school education and college educated workers earned a significant wage premium, many of them employed as managers, engineers, and chemists in factories engaged in mass scale Fordist production (Goldin and Katz 2009). The number of scientists and research engineers working in industrial labs also exploded. In turn, Total Factor Productivity (TFP) grew at an unprecedented 1.29% a year between 1899 and 1941, giving American producers an edge over those from other countries.[68] By 1929, the American share of global motor vehicle exports exceeded 70% (Nelson and Wright 1992: 1945).

Figure 12 identifies the spatial distribution of patents per capita granted in 1930, near the end of this peculiarly innovative era.[69] Technological progress during the Second Industrial Revolution was geographically concentrated. A few metro areas in New York, Massachusetts, Ohio, Michigan, Illinois, Texas, California, and Washington State stood out. In these places, new companies were formed as capital became available after investors developed methods to better screen ideas with commercial potential; entrepreneurship opportunities mushroomed as employees spun off new ventures (Lamoreaux and Sokoloff 2007). R&D programs were housed in corporate labs including Eastman Kodak, B.F. Goodrich, General Electric, Dow, DuPont, Westinghouse, RCA, US Steel, Unocal, and Goodyear.

---

[67] This was made possible by the full electrification of factories with moving assembly lines and individuated (unit driven) workspaces outfitted with machines plugged into electric sockets (David 1990). In turn, after abandoning centralized line shafts and their cumbersome pulleys and belts, factories transformed their layouts and workflows. This made manufacturing more flexible and efficient and reduced capital outlays.

[68] See Bakker, Crafts, and Woltjer (2017). While Gordon (2016) argues that gangbusters productivity growth over this period and beyond was the result of the widespread diffusion of GPTs such as electricity, Bakker, Crafts, and Woltjer (2017) disagree: they identify more of a mushroom pattern and claim that several innovations across economic sectors were responsible.

[69] Note that this is a flow variable: it is patent granted per capita in 1930, not the total stock of patents per capita granted by 1930.

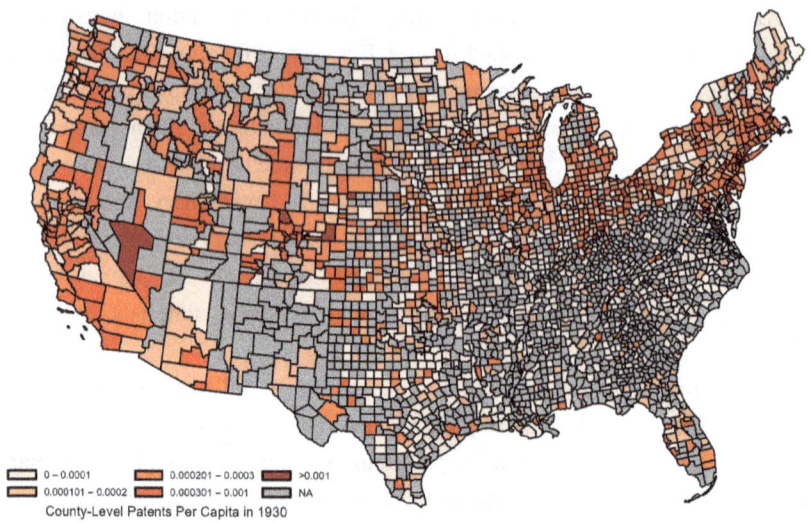

Figure 12 Patent grants per capita filed by inventors by county in 1930

Notes: We use HistPat, which spatially identifies patents granted by the USPTO from 1790 to 1975. HistPat allocates patents to each county using digitized records of original, publicly available patent documents that list the residence of the first inventor. We then divide these figures by county-level population estimates obtained from the US Census. NAs refer to counties for which HistPat does not report patent data.
Sources: Petralia, Ballard, and Rigby (2016); US Census (1930).

The similarity between the spatial patterns depicted by this map and Figure 3 in Section 2, which showcases patents per capita in 2000, is striking. Places that were innovation clusters in 1930 tend to be innovation clusters at the turn of the twenty-first century. Many of the places that pioneered the Second Industrial Revolution seamlessly welcomed the computer era and the space race. A linear regression estimated via OLS corroborates this visual correlation: an increase in counties' granted patents by 1% in 1930 maps onto an increase of 0.65% in counties' per capita granted patents in 2000 (p-value < 0.001).[70]

The Third Industrial Revolution witnessed innovation in several hardware and software based high-tech industries, with semiconductors leading the way. It began as a sequel to the Second Industrial Revolution in terms of vertically integrated companies that conducted intensive R&D in research parks. Notable contributions to innovation were developed at AT&T's Bell Labs, Xerox PARC, various IBM research labs, and Hewlett Packard's Laboratories.

---

[70] To calculate this regression, we log each variable and cluster the standard errors by commuting zone. There are 1,688 observations.

Eventually, a vertically disintegrated and global supply chain evolved.[71] First was the advent of the personal computer stack: the separation of microprocessors from hardware and from software embodied by the Wintel system. In this system, Intel both designed and manufactured the chips, IBM and several clones, such as Dell Computers, manufactured the actual personal computer, and Microsoft, as well as other software companies, designed and distributed the operating system and ancillary applications.

Second was the horizontalization of semiconductors themselves, with most chip design occurring in the United States by companies such as Qualcomm, Nvidia, and AMD, and most production offshored to East Asia, most prominently Taiwan and South Korea. Third was the development of the smartphone stack (the separation of chip designers, chipmakers, handset manufacturers, the Android operating system, and outside developers). Horizontalization was accompanied by the advent of "outsourced R&D" conducted by start-ups purchased by established firms to acquire their technology and a more multinational approach to R&D based on cross-national alliances between firms.

Besides vertical integration in its early stages, the Third Industrial Revolution was like the second in several ways. It called for a highly skilled workforce specialized in capital-intensive process innovations (see Goldin and Katz 2009: 121). Central processing units based on programmable microprocessors were widely adopted throughout the US economy, bolstering overall productivity (Gordon 2017). For example, Walmart forged several innovations in supply chain management and warehousing, including the widespread use of barcodes, computer networks, and data storage, which trickled out to other firms in its industry, such as Target. These innovations allowed retailers to forecast sales with great accuracy, slash their inventories – and thus cut down on waste and reduce costs – adopt uniform standards for labeling products, and create interoperable production and sales information that could be automatically shared in a standardized manner up and down their global supply chains and between their retail outlets (see Bonacich and Hardie 2006: 108).

The Third Industrial Revolution matured across extant innovation clusters in California, Washington State, New Mexico, Texas, New England, Illinois, Virginia, Ohio, upstate New York, and other parts of the country that boast research universities and highly educated workers (see Greenstein 2010: 512). And it was characterized by innovative funding processes, for example, venture

---

[71] This industrial revolution was powered by Moore's Law, the exponential improvement in microchip performance roughly every two years per dollar spent. It was the result of rising R&D investments and continuous experimentation by semiconductor firms to cram more transistors onto an integrated circuit's surface area, thereby shrinking electronic devices, improving their processing speed, and inducing constant price reductions (see Galetovic 2021).

capital, and spinoffs that fostered continuous entrepreneurship in these clusters (Lamoreaux and Sokoloff 2007). Most importantly, for our purposes, the industries that were forged during the Second Industrial Revolution continued to exist and innovate deep into the third one. By extension, enduring innovation clusters around steel, petrochemicals, automobiles, aircraft, chemicals, and synthetics remained economically relevant, even if they were overshadowed by places such as Silicon Valley and Route 128 (see Kerr and Nanda 2013).[72]

The spatial persistence in innovation across different time intervals between 1930 and 2000 throws this into high relief. An increase in counties' per capita patent grants by 1% in 1930 maps onto an increase of 0.63% in counties' per capita patent grants in 1950 (robust p-value < 0.001). Similarly, an increase in counties' per capita patent grants by 1% in 1930 maps onto an increase of 0.76% in counties' per capita granted patents in 1990 (robust p-value < 0.001).[73]

We now have all the pieces in place to evaluate the causal relationship between the degree of innovation at the US county-level and electoral support for Trumpism. That is precisely what we do in the next section for the 2016 presidential election. In Section 8, we repeat that exercise for the 2020 presidential election, while also looking at financial support for both of Trump's presidential campaigns. In Section 9, we do so again, but focus on the relationship between spatial innovation and electoral support for Bryan during the early twentieth century and Perot at the close of it.

7 Causal Relationship between Innovation and Trumpism, 2016

This section systematically evaluates the relationship between innovation and Trumpism at the US county level during the 2016 presidential election. To investigate whether causality indeed runs from more local innovation to less local electoral support for Trump, we explore a series of regressions estimated via IV in two stages. Following the previous section, we instrument patents per

---

[72] To be sure, the Third Industrial Revolution was heavily subsidized, if not choreographed, by the US federal government. Starting in World War II, the military oversaw the development of computers that could crack encrypted messages and sought to develop the hydrogen bomb. During the Cold War, Washington, DC awarded billions of dollars in grants to universities and labs for basic scientific research that culminated in the development of radar, lasers, semiconductors, GPS, and hardware. Military-led procurement efforts around precision-guided weapons subsidized semiconductor firms' efforts to obtain scale; as did spending by NASA on the so-called Space Race. Moreover, the federal government and military helped to develop the internet by, among other things, encouraging standards that facilitated interoperability. In Section 9 we discuss how, despite the efforts we outlined earlier in this section to even the innovation playing field between places, Washington D.C.'s industrial policies reinforced extant technology clusters and paved the way for the recrudescence of geographic innovation inequality.

[73] To calculate these regressions, we log each variable and cluster the standard errors by commuting zone. There are 1,286 observations and 1,699 observations, respectively.

capita with Precipitation and Temperature and their interaction (all measured in 1900) and log(Population Density), measured in 1900. The latter helps us isolate reasons other than a temperate climate for innovation clustering during America's industrialization, such as larger labor and consumer markets (Khalifa 2022: 29).

7.1 Econometric Strategy

To assess the causal spatial relationship between innovation and electoral support for Trump, we first revisit Table 1, Column 1, which reports the bivariate relationship estimated via OLS between log(Patents Per Capita) measured in 2000 and Trumpism. We remind readers that we first introduced this regression in the previous section. Increasing Per Capita Patents by 1% maps onto a decrease in Trumpism of 1.19 percentage points (p-value < 0.001).[74] How can we ascertain whether this correlation is a causal one?

We proceed in several steps. As a first step, we can do so by estimating IV models.[75] As a second step, we can conduct diagnostics that increase our confidence that the instruments satisfy the exclusion restriction. As a third step, we control for a host of variables whose omission may confound the main results. As a fourth step, we rule out violations of the exclusion restriction by controlling for several alternative pathways through which our instruments might influence Trump's electoral appeal in both 2016 and 2020.

We begin by describing the structure of our IV regressions and introduce and explain both our IV diagnostics and direct tests of whether the exclusion restriction is satisfied further ahead, within the context of the discussion of

---

[74] There are 189 counties missing patents data (for which we could not ascertain the number of patents granted) compared to the data coverage for Trumpism (6% of observations). Texas accounts for a relatively large number: we lack data on this variable for 40 Texan counties. We note, however, that the results hold if we omit Texas from the analyses altogether or if we interpolate the missing values in different ways, including coding them as 0s. If we treat these missing observations as 0s and rerun the regression represented by Table 1, Column 1, we obtain essentially the same coefficient on innovation, albeit with an even stronger t-statistic (4.93 for 3,104 observations versus 4.79 for 2,918 observations). Moreover, the mean and median for Trumpism is essentially the same across both the uncensored sample and the sample for which we are not missing patent observations. We also note that for the 2,918 patent observations that are not missing data there are 858 true 0s (we were able to ascertain that in fact no patents were granted), for which we add 1×10^{-9} before logging; going forward, this is our strategy for addressing patent data of any vintage that is truly 0 before logging. However, the results of this and the ensuing regressions do not materially change if we instead abstain from logging the patent data (enter it in levels), or if we add larger, yet still trivial, values before logging, or if we perform a hyperbolic sine transformation to the patents per capita values while keeping the zeroes intact.

[75] We note that the results from the bivariate regression estimated via OLS hold if we rerun the model estimated via OLS with state fixed effects or if we rerun the model estimated via OLS with state fixed effects and the various control variables we discuss and experiment with further next.

our statistical results. The first stage estimates the determinants of log(Per Capita Patents) using excluded instruments. The second stage estimates the determinants of Trumpism. We follow Autor et al. (2020) and both cluster the standard errors by commuting zone (addressing spatial correlation between counties in encompassing metro areas) and weigh the observations by counties' total votes in the 2000 presidential election.[76] For the second-stage regression, the most important thing to note is whether the predicted values of patents per capita calculated from the first stage regression explain the variation in Trumpism.

The first stage regression of our IV model with controls is:

$$w_i = \alpha_j + \beta \mathbf{X}_i + \xi(\phi_i + \lambda_i + \phi_i \times \lambda_i) + \pi(\psi_i) + u_i \tag{1}$$

Here, w_i is the estimated value of log(Patents per Capita) for county i; α_j identifies invariant state-fixed effects potentially correlated with $\mathbf{X}$, a vector of k explanatory variables in 2000 associated with β estimated parameters; ξ are estimates associated with ϕ_i, county Temperature in 1900, λ_i, county Precipitation in 1900, and their interaction (Temperature in 1900*Precipitation in 1900); π are estimates of ψ_i, county Population Density in 1900 (in logs); and u_i is an error term.

The second stage of the model is:

$$y_i = \alpha_j + \beta \mathbf{X}_i + u_i \tag{2}$$

Here, y_i is the estimated value of Trumpism for county i; α_j addresses invariant state-fixed effects potentially correlated with $\mathbf{X}$, a vector of k explanatory variables that include the predicted values of patents per capita produced by equation (1); β are estimated parameters; and u_i is an error term.

7.2 Simple to Complex Regression Approach

Before estimating the model estimated via IV in Table 1, Column 8, we discuss several simpler models. We proceed from the simplest specification to the most complex.

In Column 2a, we report the first stage regression results of our regression estimated via IV: we introduce a simple version of equation (1) that excludes

---

[76] The results are robust to an IV estimation that clusters the standard errors by state, as well as an OLS estimation that applies the spatial correction pioneered by Conley (1999). Using that approach, we experimented with different thresholds where the error term of each county was assumed to be correlated with those of all other counties located within a radius of different distances: 50 km, 100 km, 200 km, and 500 km. This meant constructing a binary variance covariance matrix with county-pairs coded as a "1" for the two counties located within the distance threshold and "0" otherwise. We also tried specifications with a distance linear decay function by applying weights in the matrix that linearly decrease as distance increases: near counties received values close to one and counties close to the distance cutoff received zeroes.

control variables and state-fixed effects. That is, we instrument log(Patents Per Capita) with Temperature, Precipitation, and Population Density, all measured in 1900. In Column 2b, we report the second-stage results. The only variable in that equation (equation 2) is the estimate (predicted values) of log(Per Capita Patents) generated by the first stage regression (equation 1). Column 2a corroborates our expectations for the first stage regression.[77]

First, there is a positive relationship between a temperate climate and innovation: The interaction between Temperature and Precipitation is negative (p-value = 0.002); the effect of increased rainfall on patents per capita in 2000 is positive only at relatively low to moderate temperatures. Increasing precipitation by 1 inch at an average temperature of 33.7 degrees in 1900 increases patents per person in 2000 by almost 5% (statistically significant at the 95% level); once average temperature crosses 55 degrees, however, the relationship between more rainfall and innovation turns negative (statistically significant at the 95% level). For example, at the highest average temperature, 74.8 degrees, a 1-inch increase in precipitation decreases patents per capita by 7% (statistically significant at the 95% level).[78]

Second, greater population density in the past maps onto greater innovation. Increasing population density by 1% in 1900 leads to a 32% increase in patents per capita in 2000 (p-value < 0.001).

Column 2b corroborates our expectations for the second-stage regression. Innovation leads to less Trumpism: increasing log(Patents Per Capita) by 1% decreases Trump's share of the 2016 two-party presidential vote by 2.22 percentage points vis-à-vis Bush's vote share in 2000 (p-value = 0.001). The r-squared of that bivariate regression is .06. This coefficient is double the one obtained when we estimate the regression via OLS (see Table 1, Column 1), which corroborates the fear, outlined in the previous section, that a simple linear

---

[77] In terms of the strength of our instruments, we note that for the first stage regression, the Partial R-squared is .05 and the F-statistic is 8.74, just shy of the threshold (10.0) for "reliable" instruments put forth by Stock, Wright, and Yogo (2002). However, Column 9 reports regression results for our Column 8 model estimated via a limited information maximum likelihood estimator (LIML) in which our main findings are materially unchanged (compared to Column 8, an IV regression estimated in two stages for the same model). The LIML is a linear combination of OLS and IV estimates, with the weights (approximately) eliminating any bias introduced by an IV regression with weak instruments (see Hahn and Hausman 2003). Moreover, the F-statistic for that first stage regression is 9.7.

[78] Consider three tropical states that fit that bill: Florida, Louisiana, and Alabama. Florida's annual rainfall in 1900 was 63 inches and its average temperature was 70 degrees; Louisiana's annual rainfall in 1900 was 65.5 inches and its average temperature was 67 degrees; Alabama's annual rainfall in 1900 was 67.5 inches and average temperature was 63.6 degrees. Each of these readings is well above the mean and median values for both Precipitation and Temperature. Compared to the average for US states in 2000, which was 0.14 per thousand people, Florida's patents per capita that year were 0.12, Louisiana's 0.07, and Alabama's 0.07.

regression may underestimate the negative effect of innovation on Trumpism. This, therefore, justifies an IV estimation strategy.[79]

We now review the results of a regression estimated via OLS that suggests that the mechanism behind our causal identification strategy is sound. The dependent variable in Column 3 is log(Biomass), measured in 2012.[80] The independent variables are Temperature, Precipitation, their interaction, and Population Density, all measured in 1900. First, there is a positive relationship between a temperate climate and biomass. As in the first stage regression of the IV estimation reported in Column 2a, where the dependent variable is log(Patents Per Capita) measured in 2000, the interaction between Temperature and Precipitation is negative (p-value = 0.002); the effect of increased rainfall on log(Biomass) is positive only at relatively low to moderate temperatures. Second, greater population density in the past maps onto greater biomass today. Increasing population density by 1% in 1900 leads to a 14% increase in biomass in 2012 (p-value = 0.001).

Might it be the case that our exclusion restriction is not satisfied, however? In the remainder of this section, we experiment with a variety of diagnostics and alternative specifications to ascertain if this is the case. That includes running tests that can help us establish whether our main results are robust to relaxing the assumption that the instrumental variables work only through innovation to affect support for Trump; we instead test the idea that they may have direct impacts on this outcome. It also includes introducing a host of control variables and state-fixed effects that are potential confounders: may be correlated with patents per capita. Finally, we also experiment with directly introducing potential alternative pathways connecting our demographic, geographic, and climatic instruments to electoral support for Trump into the IV regressions.

As a first step, we turn to a Plausibly Exogenous Instrument Test (see Conley, Hansen, and Rosen 2012). To grasp its logic and technicalities, first consider the following reduced-form model:

$$y_i = \beta X_i + \xi(\phi_i + \lambda_i + \phi_i \times \lambda_i) + \pi(\psi_i) + u_i \qquad (3)$$

Here, y_i is the value of Trumpism for county i; X_i is log(Patents Per Capita) for county i; ξ are estimates associated with ϕ_i, county Temperature in 1900,

---

[79] We note that this difference in coefficients between the regression estimated via OLS and the one estimated via IV is not a by-product of the fewer observations associated with the latter because of missing data for the instruments. The results of the regression estimated via OLS hold if we restrict the observations to be identical to those associated with Column 2b.

[80] The results reported in Column 4 hold if we instead measure biomass as log(Biomass/Surface Area).

λ_i, county Precipitation in 1900, and their interaction; π are estimates of ψ_i, county Population Density in 1900 (in logs); and u_i is an error term.

If the exclusion restriction is satisfied in equation (3), then a reduced form regression estimated via OLS, and that includes both the potentially endogenous regressor and its instruments simultaneously, should yield coefficients on the instruments that are precisely zero. Such a result would allow us to surmise that they work exclusively through the potentially endogenous regressor to affect the dependent variable.

Rather than assuming the instruments' coefficients are precisely equal to 0 in the reduced form equation, however, we now follow the Plausibly Exogenous Instrument Test pioneered by Conley, Hansen, and Rosen (2012). Their framework allows the exclusion restriction to fail in an IV estimation and, thus, assumes that the coefficients on the instruments deviate from zero. We opt for conducting a sensitivity analysis for the effect of patents on support for Trump in 2016 using the Localized to Zero (LTZ) approach within the Plausibly Exogenous Instrument Test framework (see Conley, Hansen, and Rosen 2012). Gamma (γ) represents the degree of violation of the exclusion restriction assumption. It quantifies the extent to which the instruments (Z) have a direct effect on the outcome variable (Y), beyond its effect through the endogenous variable (X).

To put this more directly, because we have four instruments as represented by ξ in equation (3), we estimate the effect of patents per capita on Trumpism after imposing four unique γ values associated with ϕ_i, λ_i, π, and ψ_i in that equation. Therefore, as γ increases its deviation from zero, it implies a larger violation of the exclusion restriction assumption because Z is assumed to have a stronger direct effect on Y. The LTZ approach requires that we specify a distribution that describes our prior belief about γ for each instrument. Following convention, we assume that each γ (that is, ϕ_i, λ_i, π, and ψ_i) is normally distributed with mean μ and variance ω (see Conley, Hansen, and Rosen 2012).

To establish some priors on how our instruments may have a direct effect on support for Trump, we pursue two strategies. The first is theoretical (a priori) and the second empirical (a posteriori). In terms of the theoretical approach, we discipline our priors about the γ values using some reasonable conjectures informed by the literature and what we already know about the world. This allows us to both simulate how manipulating both the potential direct effects (operationalized as μ) in different ways and the uncertainty about these effects (ω) impacts the effect of patents on Trumpism. In terms of the empirical approach, our priors about μ are simply the coefficients obtained by estimating equation (3) via OLS (ϕ_i, λ_i, π, and ψ_i) and ω are these estimated coefficients' variances.

First, whatever conditions influenced population density in the past might reasonably also predict population density today and population density in 1900 might work through population density today. This matters because more progressive people may flock to denser areas or the denizens of dense cities may become more liberal over time. Therefore, we experiment with relaxing the assumption that the exclusion restriction holds for Population Density in 1900 and assume it has a direct, negative effect on Trumpism.

Second, places that are hotter, or more humid, or that experience more climate extremes, may increase voters' concerns over climate change. In turn, climate change may be more politically salient and may translate into less support for Trump. Or perhaps an additional potential channel by which the past climate might affect Trumpism is through a culture of cooperation and other concerning morality (Buggle and Durante 2021; Giuliano and Nunn 2021). Therefore, we experiment with relaxing the assumption that the exclusion restriction holds for Temperature in 1900 and assume it has a direct, negative effect on Trumpism.

To be sure, these are not the only potential direct effects of our instruments on Trumpism. However, because we do not have strong priors about the direct effects of either precipitation on support for Trump or how precipitation may compound any direct effect of temperature on support for Trump, we do not report results where we assume nonzero values for μ for that set of instruments. However, we note that our main results are robust to relaxing this assumption. First, experimenting with different μ and ω values for Precipitation in 1900 and for Temperature in 1900*Precipitation in 1900 yields materially similar results. Second, we demonstrate that if we assume that the μ and ω values for our instruments are those obtained by a reduced form regression estimated via OLS as depicted by equation (3), the effect of patents per capita on Trumpism remains both substantively and statistically significant. Third, we demonstrate that this also holds true when we directly introduce a bevy of potential alternative pathways connecting our demographic, geographic, and climatic instruments to electoral support for Trump directly into the IV regressions.

Table 2 reports how the point estimate and 95% confidence intervals for the estimated effect of patents on support for Trump change as our prior for the distribution of the direct effect of some of the instruments varies. These results are obtained from a series of Plausibly Exogenous Instrument regressions that use the LTZ approach. Across Panel A, we vary either μ or ω for Population Density in 1900 and assume that μ and ω for the other instruments are 0. In Columns 1 to 3, we vary μ for Population Density in 1900 and hold ω proportional to the μ value at a 1:3.75 inverse ratio; this assumes relatively

Table 2 Point estimates and confidence intervals for Trumpism varying μ and ω for factors in Z

PANEL A

Parameter manipulated	(1) μ	(2) μ	(3) μ	(4) ω	(5) Ω
log(Patents Per Capita, 2000)	−1.72	−1.23	−0.73	−1.72	−1.72
95% Confidence Intervals	[−2.61, −0.84]	[−2.34, −0.09]	[−2.07, 0.61]	[−3.38, −0.07]	[−3.52, 0.08]
Temperature μ value	0	0	0	0	0
Temperature ω value	0	0	0	0	0
Precipitation μ value	0	0	0	0	0
Precipitation ω value	0	0	0	0	0
Temperature X Precipitation μ value	0	0	0	0	0
Temperature X Precipitation ω value	0	0	0	0	0
Population Density μ value	−0.5	−1	−1.5	−0.5	−0.5
Population Density ω value	0.13	0.27	0.4	0.65	0.78

PANEL B

Parameter manipulated	(6) μ	(7) μ	(8) μ	(9) ω	(10) Ω
log(Patents Per Capita, 2000)	−2.06	−1.91	−1.43	−2.06	−2.06
95% Confidence Intervals	[−2.94, −1.18]	[−3.03, −0.77]	[−3.11, 0.26]	[−3.19, −0.93]	[−6.03, 1.91]
Temperature μ value	−0.05	−0.1	−0.25	−0.05	−0.05
Temperature ω value	0.01	0.03	0.07	0.03	0.04
Precipitation μ value	0	0	0	0	0
Precipitation ω value	0	0	0	0	0
Temperature X Precipitation μ value	0	0	0	0	0

Table 2 (cont.)

Temperature X Precipitation ω value	0	0	0	0
Population Density μ value	0	0	0	0
Population Density ω value	0	0	0	0
PANEL C	(11)		(12)	
Parameter manipulated	μ		μ	
log(Patents Per Capita, 2000)	−1.56		−0.91	
95% Confidence Intervals	[−2.7, −0.43]		[−2.42, 0.61]	
Temperature μ value	−0.05		−0.1	
Temperature ω value	0.01		0.03	
Precipitation μ value	0		0	
Precipitation ω value	0		0	
Temperature X Precipitation μ value	0		0	
Temperature X Precipitation ω value	0		0	
Population Density μ value	−0.5		−1	
Population Density ω value	0.13		0.27	

Notes: the table reports parameter estimates and 95% confidence intervals for a sensitivity analysis using the LTZ approach in the Plausibly Exogenous Instruments Framework for the case where we vary our prior for the direct effect of either/both Population Density in 1900 and Temperature in 1900 on support for Trump. The log(Patents Per Capita, 2000) row reports the 2SLS coefficient estimate of patents per capita (β) on support for Trump at different values of μ and ω. Following Conley, Hansen, and Rossi (2012), we assume a normal distribution for μ (the mean of γ) with variance ω. Following Autor et al. (2020), we calculate "Trumpism" by subtracting the two-party Republican vote share in 2000 from the two-party Republican vote share in 2016. Like they do, we exclude Alaska and Hawaii because of missing data. We cluster the standard errors across all models by commuting zone and weigh the observations by counties' total votes in the 2000 presidential election.

tight confidence bounds around the point estimate for γ. In Columns 4 to 5, we vary ω for Population Density in 1900 and assume a constant μ, which we set to -0.5. Across Panel B, we vary either μ or ω for Temperature in 1900 and assume that μ and ω for the other instruments are 0. In Columns 6 to 8, we vary μ for Temperature in 1900 and hold ω proportional to the μ value at a 1:3.75 inverse ratio, which assumes relatively tight confidence bounds around the point estimate for γ. In Columns 9 to 10, we vary ω for Temperature in 1900 and assume a constant μ, which we set to -0.05. In Panel C, we vary μ for both Population Density in 1900 and Temperature in 1900 and assume that μ and ω for the other instruments are 0. For both instruments we hold ω proportional to their respective μ values at a 1:3.75 inverse ratio in these regressions, again assuming relatively tight confidence bounds around the point estimates for γ. Next we explain the results reported in Table 2.

In Panel A, Column 1 we make a relatively conservative assumption about the μ for Population Density in 1900, and set it to equal -0.5, with ω equal to 0.13. Increasing patents per capita by 1% reduces support for Trump by 1.72 percentage points, a point estimate that remains comfortably within the negative range across both its lower and upper 95% confidence intervals. However, this is 23% smaller than the coefficient obtained in Table 1, Column 2b, a cognate IV regression that assumes no deviation from the exclusion restriction. This suggests that while our main result is somewhat sensitive to assuming that population density in 1900 has a direct effect on Trumpism, it is nonetheless resilient to a nontrivial violation of the exclusion restriction. In Column 2 we set μ to -1, with ω equal to 0.27. Increasing patents per capita by 1% now reduces support for Trump by 1.23 percentage points, which nonetheless remains negative across both its lower and upper 95% confidence intervals. However, in Column 3, when we set μ to -1.5, with ω equal to 0.4, we learn that if we assume that a 1% increase in Population Density in 1900 reduces support for Trump by 1.5 percentage points, our main result is no longer statistically significant at conventional levels. While increasing patents per capita by 1% reduces support for Trump by 0.73 percentage points, the lower bound of the effect now crosses into positive territory. However, considering that the average value of the *level* of Trumpism in the sample is only 7.7, the effect of patents per capita on support for Trump is only undermined when the IV regression encounters an appreciable violation of the exclusion restriction.

A similar pattern holds when we increase the uncertainty around the direct effect of population density in 1900 by a relatively large amount. First, as in Column 1, in Column 4 we set μ to equal -0.5. However, we now quintuple ω, increasing it from 0.13 to 0.65. While the point estimate for patents per capita obtained in Column 1 weakens, its lower bound remains below 0. In other words, our main result is robust to this manipulation of the variance of the direct effect of population density in 1900. However, once we sextuple ω, setting it to 0.78, then the lower bound of the effect of patents per capita on Trumpism now crosses into positive territory (see Column 5).

In Panel B, Column 6 we make a relatively conservative assumption about the μ of Temperature in 1900 and set it to equal -0.05, with ω equal to 0.013. Increasing patents per capita by 1% reduces support for Trump by 2.06 percentage points, a point estimate that remains comfortably within the negative range across both its lower and upper 95% confidence intervals. This is only 7% smaller than the coefficient obtained in Table 1, Column 2b, a cognate IV regression that assumes no deviation from the exclusion restriction. This suggests that while our main result is somewhat sensitive to assuming that Temperature in 1900 has a direct effect on Trumpism, it is nonetheless resilient to a nontrivial violation of the exclusion restriction. In Column 7 we set μ to −0.10, with ω equal to 0.027. Increasing patents per capita by 1% now reduces support for Trump by 1.91 percentage points, which nonetheless remains negative across both its lower and upper 95% confidence intervals. However, in Column 8, when we set μ to −0.25, with ω equal to 0.066, we learn that while increasing patents per capita by 1% reduces support for Trump by 1.43 percentage points, the lower bound of the effect now crosses into positive territory. We therefore learn that if we allow Temperature in 1900 to have a direct effect on Trumpism whereby increasing it by one degree Fahrenheit reduces support for Trump by 0.25 percentage points, our main result is no longer statistically significant at conventional levels.

A similar pattern again holds when we increase the uncertainty around this direct effect. In Column 9, if we set μ for temperature in 1900 to equal −0.5, and double ω (compared to Column 6), going from 0.013 to 0.026, then the point estimate for patents per capita weakens, but its lower bound remains below 0. However, once we triple ω, setting it to 0.04, then the lower bound estimate of the effect of patents per capita on Trumpism now crosses into positive territory (see Column 10).

What happens if we hypothesize that both population density in 1900 and temperature in 1900 have a direct effect on Trumpism simultaneously? In Panel A, Column 11 we set the μ for population density in 1900 to −0.5, with ω equal to 0.13, and set the μ for Temperature in 1900 to −0.05, with ω equal to 0.013. Increasing patents per capita by 1% reduces support for Trump by 1.56 percentage points, a point estimate that remains comfortably within the negative range across both its lower and upper 95% confidence intervals. However, this is 30% smaller than the coefficient obtained in Table 1, Column 2b, a cognate IV regression that assumes no deviation from the exclusion restriction. This suggests that while our main result is somewhat sensitive to assuming that both Population Density in 1900 and Temperature in 1900 have a direct effect on Trumpism, it is nonetheless resilient to a nontrivial violation of the exclusion restriction. In Column 12, we set the µ for Population Density in 1900 to −1, with ω equal to 0.266, and set the µ for temperature in 1900 to −0.10, with ω equal to 0.027. Increasing patents per capita by 1% now reduces support for Trump by only 0.91 percentage points. Moreover, the lower bound of the effect crosses into positive territory. This specification again ratifies the notion that there are limits to violating the exclusion restriction: if both population density in 1900 and temperature in 1900 both have a direct, negative effect on Trumpism simultaneously, then it is more likely that innovation does not systematically reduce support for Trump across all samples when their respective µ's are relatively large.

We hasten to emphasize that while we do not have strong priors about the direct effects of either precipitation on support for Trump or how precipitation may compound any direct effect of temperature on support for Trump, there is the possibility that they both have a direct effect on Trumpism. There is also the possibility that the direct effects of Temperature in 1900 and Population Density in 1900 are different from those we simulated earlier. Therefore, we now inform our priors strictly "empirically" by assuming that the µ and ω values for our instruments in the Plausibly Exogenous Instrument Test are those obtained by a reduced form regression estimated via OLS as depicted by equation (3).[81] After estimating such a regression, we learn that ϕ_i, λ_i, π, and ψ_i are −0.263, 0.113, 0.009, and −0.718, respectively, and their variances are 0.004, 0.003, 0, and 0.053, respectively.

The effect of patents per capita on Trumpism remains both substantively and statistically significant after conducting this experiment: Increasing patents per capita by 1% reduces support for Trump by 1.89 percentage points, a point estimate that remains comfortably within the negative range across both its lower and upper 95% confidence intervals, which are −2.65 and −1.14, respectively. This suggests that while our main result is somewhat sensitive to assuming that each of our instruments has a direct effect on Trumpism, it is nonetheless resilient to a nontrivial violation of the exclusion restriction.

Additionally, we now turn to the Imperfect Instrument Test developed by Nevo and Rosen (2012) to ensure that our results are robust to a different diagnostic technique. We now assume that X_i are potentially endogenous and

---

[81] To obtain the correct marginal effects for Temperature in 1900 and Precipitation in 1900 we estimate this regression after centering the constituent terms in the Temperature in 1900*Precipitation in 1900 interaction term: we subtract their respective values from their respective mean values.

$\phi_i, \lambda_i, \phi_i \times \lambda_i$, and ψ_i are instruments that are correlated with u_i. We further assume that the correlation between $\phi_i, \lambda_i, \phi_i \times \lambda_i$, and ψ_i and u_i has the same sign as the correlation between X_i and u_i and that the instrumental variables are less correlated with the error term than is log(Patents Per Capita). Under these assumptions, the Imperfect Instrument Test calculates both lower and upper estimate bounds for β.[82] If we estimate those bounds using the Imperfect Instrument Test with bootstrapped standard errors, we obtain bounds for the log(Per Capita Patent) coefficient between −2.648 and −0.676, with confidence intervals between −5.705 and −0.558. If we compare this with the coefficient returned for this variable in Column 2b, which is −2.219, with −3.488 and −0.950 confidence intervals (95%), this strongly vindicates the original IV estimates.

We now consider whether omitted variables may confound the negative relationship between innovation and Trumpism represented by Column 2b. Therefore, we turn to a series of less restrictive IV regressions estimated in two stages to address this possibility. These are reported in the rest of Table 1, where we report the second-stage results of various models.

As a first step, we consider that Autor et al. (2020) argue that increased (local) import competition from China after 2000 explains greater support for Trump during the 2016 elections. It may be the case that more innovation in 2000 unduly proxies for a smaller Chinese trade shock. To find out if this is true, in Column 4 we control for the county-level change in Chinese import exposure per worker between 2000 and 2008. This is how Autor et al. (2020) measure the Chinese trade shock; they argue this shift share measure captures the extent to which local labor markets were faced with competition from Chinese imports during this period.[83] Compared to the bivariate specification in Column 2b (the second-stage regression of our initial IV estimation), our

---

[82] Nevo and Rosen (2012) argue that to obtain two-sided bounds on the endogenous regressor's coefficient they need to make two straightforward assumptions. First, stronger restrictions on the correlation of the observables than the conventional IV estimation, as well as a weaker assumption about the unobservables than that approach (a nonzero correlation between the instruments and the error term). Second, the correlation between the instrumental variables and the error term must be assumed less than the correlation between the endogenous variable and the error term, which is required by an IV estimation over an OLS estimation. This then allows them to set boundaries for the degree of correlation between the instrumental variables and the error term between 0 and the actual correlation of the endogenous regressor and the error term.

[83] Specifically, the authors estimate the change in ad valorem US imports from China within a given locality in real dollars and then divide this value by the number of workers in each location. They use trade data from the UN Comtrade dataset, obtaining the dollar value of net imports across different industries. They aggregate industry imports to the commuting zone level, and ultimately the county, according to industries' local share of national employment. They then divide by the total workers in a location, which they estimate by aggregating up industry wide data on employment to commuting zones and then counties.

substantive and statistical results strengthen somewhat. The localized China Trade Shock variable is, as in Autor et al. (2020), positive and statistically significant. Its point estimate (2.072; p-value = 0.02) suggests that an interquartile range change (of 0.567) in this variable increases Trumpism by 1.18 percentage points.

What happens if, as Autor et al. (2020) do, we instrument localized China Trade Shock with a shift-share instrument in the first stage regression? The latter is constructed by the authors as the initial shares of employment in a given location and industry multiplied by the growth of Chinese imports in eight developed countries (Australia, Denmark, Finland, Germany, Japan, New Zealand, Spain, and Switzerland) during the same time window.[84] According to Autor et al. (2020), this approach captures the exogenous variation in Chinese import exposure per worker (it isolates the portion of US county growth in Chinese imports driven by increased competitiveness: excludes the share driven by idiosyncratic increases in import demand).

Column 5 reveals that this experiment produces materially similar results. Patents Per Capita's predictive value is now stronger, in both substantive and statistical terms. As expected, the China Trade Shock variable also strengthens once we isolate its exogenous variation: the coefficient increases by 67%. Therefore, in the regressions that follow, we continue to control for Chinese import exposure per worker instrumented with its shift share in the ensuing first-stage regressions (see equation 1). For now, we surmise that, while there may be a strong, positive relationship between exposure to increased Chinese imports after 2000 and Trumpism in 2016, there is also a strong, negative relationship between innovation and Trumpism.

As a second step, in Column 6 we introduce state-fixed effects. These capture the state-invariant, unobserved heterogeneity that is correlated with both Patents Per Capita in 2000 and Trumpism. Our results are much stronger, experiencing a three-fold rise in magnitude (increasing patents per capita by 1% engenders a 6.1 percentage point decrease in the Republican Party's vote share in 2016 versus 2000; p-value < 0.001).

As a third step, following Autor et al. (2020), in Column 7 we add a host of baseline county-level controls. While the authors provide the full explanation and sources for those variables in Table 5 of that paper, we discuss them at some

---

[84] Autor et al. (2020) document that all eight comparison countries experienced import growth from China in 343 of 397 four-digit SIC manufacturing industries and that import patterns across these countries' industries are highly correlated with the patterns in US industries. Autor et al. (2020) use bilateral trade data from the UN Comtrade Database to calculate US import values, which they convert to real dollars, and crosswalk this information to four-digit SIC industries. As with their China Shock variable, they measure employment by industry at the commuting zone.

length here as well. First are industry and occupation controls from the 2000 County Business Patterns data, which include employment in the manufacturing sector; second are the share of occupations that involve routinized work (and can be potentially automated) and the share of occupations that can be outsourced overseas, both from Autor and Dorn (2013). Third are census division dummies. Fourth are demographic controls that measure the share of the population across different age groups, races, gender, education levels, and immigration status (all these are measured in 2000 and come from the 2000 US Census). Finally, we include election controls that measure the Republican two-party vote share in the 1992 and 1996 presidential elections from David Leip's Election Atlas. While the substantive effect of patents per capita is weakened after we include all these control variables, it remains statistically significant at the highest possible level.[85] Table 3 provides summary statistics of these "baseline" control variables and some additional controls we discuss next.

Column 8 introduces more county-level variables beyond those included in Autor et al. (2020). We add log(Real Median Income Per Capita) in 1999 from the 2000 US Census. We also add the Unemployment Rate in 2000 from the USDA Economic Research Service. Finally, we also control for how rural a location is using Waldorf and Kim's (2015) Rurality Index. Introducing these controls strengthens the substantive and statistical significance of our main result: innovation continues to appreciably reduce support for Trumpism at the highest level of statistical significance.

Column 9 addresses the possibility that the instruments for log(Patents Per Capita) contained across the first stage regressions in the IV estimations (equation 1) are weak. It reports the regression results from an LIML estimator, a linear combination of OLS and IV estimates, with the weights (approximately) eliminating any bias introduced by an IV regression estimated in two stages with weak instruments (see Hahn and Hausman 2003); the model is otherwise identical in terms of the variables included in Column 8. Compared to Column 8, patents per capita are considerably stronger in both a substantive and statistical sense.

7.3 Robustness to Potential Violations of the Exclusion Restriction

Even though our main IV results are robust to introducing all manner of control variables and state-fixed effects, there is the possibility that our exclusion

---

[85] These results hold after introducing interaction terms between the localized China Trade Shock variable and variables theorized by some researchers to condition its impact on support for Trumpism. First, the percent of the population that is white. Second, the percent of the population that is college educated. Third, whether the county is in the so-called Rust Belt. Third, a triple interaction term between China Trade Shock, Percent White, and Percent College Educated.

Table 3 Descriptive statistics for control variables in regression models 7–9

Variable	Average	Stand. Dev.	Min	Max
Pop. Share 10–19	0.15	0.02	0.07	0.32
Pop. Share 20–29	0.12	0.03	0.03	0.36
Pop. Share 30–39	0.14	0.02	0.06	0.23
Pop. Share 40–49	0.15	0.01	0.06	0.28
Pop. Share 50–59	0.12	0.02	0.02	0.23
Pop. Share 60–69	0.09	0.02	0.02	0.19
Pop. Share 70–79	0.07	0.02	0.01	0.17
Pop. Share 80 and over	0.04	0.02	0.00	0.12
Manufact. Employment Share	0.20	0.10	0.00	0.55
Pop. Share Female	0.50	0.02	0.33	0.57
Pop. Share College	0.43	0.11	0.17	0.85
Pop. Share Foreign Born	0.03	0.05	0.00	0.51
Pop. Share White	0.85	0.16	0.05	1.00
Pop. Share Black	0.09	0.15	0.00	0.86
Pop. Share Asian	0.01	0.02	0.00	0.31
Pop. Share Hispanic	0.06	0.12	0.00	0.98
Task Outsourcing Index	−0.50	0.47	−1.64	1.24
Rep. Vote Share 1992	0.50	0.11	0.10	0.89
Rep. Vote Share 1996	0.50	0.12	0.10	0.88
Rurality Index 2000	0.51	0.10	0.04	0.76
Unemployment Rate 2000	0.04	0.02	0.01	0.17
Routine Occupation Index	2,964	282	2,223	3,666
Median Per Capita Income 1999	35,273	8,850	12,692	82,929

Sources: Demographic variables are from the 2000 US Census and are all measured in 2000. The Manufacturing Employment Share is from the 2000 County Business Patterns data. Routine Occupation and Task Outsourcing indices come from Autor and Dorn (2013). The Republican two-party vote share in the presidential elections of 1992 and 1996 is from David Leip's Election Atlas. The Rurality Index for the year 2000 is from Waldorf and Kim (2015). The Median Income Per Capita in 1999 is from the 2000 US Census. The Unemployment Rate in 2000 is from the USDA Economic Research Service.

restriction is not fully satisfied. In Table 1, we experimented with several sensitivity analyses where our instruments were assumed to violate the exclusion restriction. There, we discovered that the negative effect of innovation on support for Trump remained both substantively and statistically significant in the face of relatively strong direct effects of some of our instruments on support for Trump (see Table 2, Columns 1, 2, 4, 6, 7, 9, and 11). However, this was not the case when these effects were very strong, or if we severely increased our uncertainty about them (see Table 2, Columns 3, 5, 8, 10, and 12). We therefore now attempt to further probe whether our independent variable of interest, patents per capita, continues to exhibit a causal effect even if we introduce proxies for those potential direct effects. This section and its accompanying regression table, Table 4, now evaluate potential violations of the exclusion restriction directly: We control for several alternative pathways through which our instruments might influence Trump's electoral appeal in both 2016 and 2020.

There are several potential channels through which a location's past climate, geography, and demography may have affected politics today beyond their impact on contemporary levels of innovation. First, these factor endowments may have influenced the demographic, attitudinal, and ideological makeup of different areas through sorting. More progressive people might live in denser places (Bishop 2009; Rodden 2019) and have voted against Trump. Similarly, climate, geography, and demography in the past may have influenced where universities are located, and those institutions of higher education may have shaped political attitudes, with more liberal-minded individuals drawn to colleges voting against Trump. Alternatively, these factor endowments might influence today's climate or susceptibility to meteorological events; voters who reside in hotter or more humid places, which may also experience more climate extremes, may care more about climate change, which may also translate into less support for Trump. Finally, it might be the case that past climate, geography, and demography drive the presence of capital-intensive and technologically advanced manufacturing that makes greater use of industrial robots; in turn, higher levels of automation may explain support for Trump.

To remind readers, one of our instrumental variables (see equation 2) is Population Density in 1900. Therefore, Column 1 (in Table 4) is an IV regression that is identical to Column 8, Table 1, except that it includes population density measured in 2000, using data from the US Census 2000.

The logic is that whatever past conditions influenced population density in the past might reasonably also predict population density today. Thus, our instrument might work through population density today, which might be correlated with electoral outcomes for reasons unrelated to innovation. More progressive people may flock to urban areas or the denizens of dense cities may become more liberal over time. Column 1 reveals that when controlling for population density in 2000, however, the coefficient on log(Patents Per Capita) is stronger, it is now -2.74 (p-value $= 0.001$), compared to -2.566 in Model 8 (Table 1).

Column 2 is a regression estimated via IV in two stages identical to Column 8, Table 1, except that it includes the number of evangelical adherents per capita in 2000 (from Grammich et al. 2012). The logic is that past geographic, climatic, and demographic factors may have influenced the religious beliefs and therefore

Table 4 The determinants of Trumpism and direct tests of the exclusion restriction

PANEL A

	(1)	(2)	(3)	(4)	(5)
Estimation Strategy	IV (Stage 2)	IV (Stage 2)	IV (Stage 2)	IV (Stage 2)	IV (Stage 2)
log(Patents Per Capita)	−2.74***	−2.442***	−2.614***	−2.625***	−2.0***
	[0.858]	[0.630]	[0.612]	[0.631]	[0.663]
Population Density in 2000	Yes	No	No	No	No
Evangelical Adherents P.C.	No	Yes	No	No	No
College Density	No	No	Yes	No	No
Higher Education Enrollment	No	No	No	Yes	No
Climate Change Happening	No	No	No	No	Yes
Climate Change Experience	No	No	No	No	No
Robot Exposure	No	No	No	No	No
Automation Ris	No	No	No	No	No
Shift Share Instrument Robots	No	No	No	No	No
Observations	2,653	2,653	2,653	2,653	2,653

Table 4 (cont.)

PANEL B

Estimation Strategy	(6) IV (Stage 2)	(7) IV (Stage 2)	(8) IV (Stage 2)	(9) IV (Stage 2)	(10) IV (Stage 2)
log(Patents Per Capita)	−1.577***	−2.675***	−2.791***	−2.47***	−2.221***
	[0.614]	[0.648]	[0.661]	[0.622]	[0.881]
Population Density in 2000	No	No	No	No	Yes
Evangelical Adherents P.C.	No	No	No	No	Yes
College Density	No	No	No	No	Yes
Higher Education Enrollment	No	No	No	No	Yes
Climate Change Happening	No	No	No	No	Yes
Climate Change Experience	Yes	No	No	No	Yes
Robot Exposure	No	Yes	Yes	No	Yes
Automation Risk	No	No	No	Yes	Yes
Shift Share Instrument Robots	No	No	Yes	No	Yes
Observations	2,653	2,653	2,653	2,621	2,653

Notes: Significant at the .01 level (***); significant at the 0.05 level (**); significant at the 0.10 level (*). Patents Per Capita measured in 2000. Following Autor et al. (2020), we calculate "Trumpism" by subtracting the two-party Republican vote share in 2000 from the two-party Republican vote share in 2016. Like they do, we exclude Alaska and Hawaii because of missing data. We estimate, but do not report, several first stage regression results for the models estimated via IV. We cluster the standard errors across all models by commuting zone and weigh the observations by counties' total votes in the 2000 presidential election. See text for what variables are included in both the Baseline Controls and Additional Controls, which we include across all models, along with state-fixed effects. We include the shift-share instrument for Chinese Import Exposure in the first stage across all models.

ideology of individuals living in different areas of the country today. Over both colonial and US history, many people of faith migrated to new places – the western frontier, for example – to either convert others, escape persecution, or develop communities of faith centered on the availability of cheap arable land, water, or other geographic and climatic features. Different areas within the United States also vary substantially in their diversity of different religious denominations (see Warf and Winsberg 2008).

Our instrument might thus work through the presence of evangelicals today, which might be correlated with electoral outcomes for reasons unrelated to innovation. More conservative people may seek out these communities, or the incumbent evangelicals living there already may be less liberal-leaning to start with. Moreover, increased homogeneity generally may translate into more support for Trump and our measure of evangelical adherents may also capture counties' relative religious and ideological homogeneity. Column 2 reveals that when controlling for evangelical adherents per capita, however, the coefficient on log(Patents Per Capita) remains basically unchanged, it is now −2.442 (p-value < 0.001) compared to −2.566 in Model 8 (Table 1).

Column 3 is an IV regression that is identical to Column 8, Table 1, except that it includes College Density, the number of higher education institutions per square mile of a county's surface area (from IPEDS 2021). The logic is that because past geographic, climatic, and demographic conditions influenced the location of early mining activity, agriculture, and industrialization, they may have also determined where institutions of higher education were founded and survived (see Goldin and Katz 2009). In turn, institutions of higher education may explain political attitudes today: more liberal-minded individuals who are drawn to colleges or who work in colleges or choose to live in college towns voting against Trump. Column 3 reveals that when controlling for College Density, however, the coefficient on log(Patents Per Capita) remains materially unchanged, it is now −2.614 (p-value < 0.001), compared to −2.566 in Model 8 (Table 1).

Column 4 is a regression estimated via IV that is identical to Column 8, Table 1, except that it includes Higher Education Enrollment, the number of people enrolled in higher education in 2000, which includes both college and postgraduate students (from the US Census 2000). While the logic of including this variable in the model is essentially the same as in Column 3, it could be the case that College Density has not fully captured the extent to which past geographic, climatic, and demographic factors may have influenced the sheer magnitude of the influence made by college and postgraduate students in a community. One big state college in a locality may fail to impact our measure of College Density, but its sizable student body may nonetheless represent an outsized proportion of county residents. Column 4 reveals that when controlling for Higher Education Enrollment, however, the coefficient on log(Patents Per Capita) remains materially unchanged, it is now −2.625 (p-value < 0.001), compared to −2.566 in Model 8 (Table 1).

Column 5 is a regression estimated via IV that is identical to Column 8, Table 1, except that it includes Climate Change Happening, the estimated number of people in a county strongly agreeing with the notion that Climate Change is happening in 2021 (from Howe et al. 2015). The logic is that past climate, geography, and demography plausibly influence today's climate or susceptibility to meteorological events. Places that are hotter, or more humid, or that experience more climate extremes, may increase voters' concerns over climate change. For example, residents of coastal regions may be more aware of the destructive impact of storms like 2012's Superstorm Sandy or worsening beach erosion. In turn, climate change may be more politically salient and may translate into less support for Trump. In other words, to address the possibility that our instruments work through contemporary attitudes about climate change to explain variation in support for Trump, we control climate change attitudes. Column 5 reveals that when controlling for Climate Change Happening, however, the coefficient on log(Patents Per Capita) only somewhat weakens, it is now −2.0 (p-value = 0.03), compared to −2.566 in Model 8 (Table 1).

Column 6 is a regression estimated via IV that is identical to Table 1 Column 8, except that it includes Climate Change Experience, the estimated number of people in a county who strongly agree that they have personally experienced the effects of climate change (from Howe et al. 2015). While the logic of including this variable in the model is essentially the same as in Column 5, it could be the case that Climate Change Happening does not fully capture the extent to which past geographic, climatic, and demographic factors may have influenced the political salience of climate change for residents living in specific US locations more susceptible to the negative consequences of climate change. Column 6 reveals that when controlling for Climate Change Experience, the coefficient on log(Patents Per Capita) weakens, it is now −1.576 (p-value = 0.01), compared to −2.566 in Model 8 (Table 1).[86]

Column 7 is a regression estimated via IV that is identical to Column 8, Table 1, except that it includes Robot Exposure, the average change in the local industry-level penetration of industrial robots between 2004 and 2010. This variable is based on the share of national employment according to 1990 Community Business Pattern industry data (and is from Acemoglu and

---

[86] The results of this experiment are robust to including any of the other variables on climate change opinions from Howe et al. (2015) dataset instead of Climate Change Happening or Climate Change Experience. Namely, log(Patents Per Capita) remains substantively and statistically significant in the second stage of the IV model no matter what survey question we add to the regression.

Restrepo 2020). The logic is that past geographic, climatic, and demographic conditions influenced the degree of automation in recent time periods by predisposing some places to greater degrees of capital-intensive industrialization and, in particular, technologically advanced manufacturing; in turn, higher levels of automation may explain support for Trump (Frey, Berger, and Chen 2018). Column 7 reveals that when controlling for Robot Exposure, however, the coefficient on log(Patents Per Capita) strengthens, it is now −2.675 (p-value < 0.001), compared to −2.566 in Model 8 (Table 1).

What happens if, as Frey, Berger, and Chen (2018) do, we instrument Robot Exposure with a shift-share instrument in the first stage regression? These authors use data on the change in penetration of industrial robots in 10 European countries based on industries' share of national employment according to 1980 Community Business Pattern industry data during the same time window as Robot Exposure. According to the authors and Acemoglu and Restrepo (2020), this approach captures the exogenous variation in automation per worker (isolates the portion of US county growth in automation driven by increased technological innovation generally and excludes the share driven by idiosyncratic increases in the demand for robots).[87]

Column 8 is a regression estimated via IV that is identical to Column 8, Table 1, except that it includes Robot Exposure instrumented by the variable described earlier, Robust Exposure European Analogs (we match the Robot Exposure window and measure this between 2004 and 2010). Column 8 reveals that this way of accounting for the potential endogeneity of automation strengthens the main results: the coefficient on log(Patents Per Capita) is now −2.790 (p-value < 0.001), compared to −2.566 in Model 8 (Table 1).

Might it be that we have mismeasured the risk of automation and thus discounted the possibility that our own instrumental variables, which we argue capture the exogenous variation in local innovation, potentially work instead through increased automation in both goods and services to affect electoral support for Trump in 2016? The exposure to industrial robots may not fully capture the extent to which voters might have been or fear of being

---

[87] Acemoglu and Restrepo (2020) use estimates on the average penetration of industrial robots across industries in Denmark, Finland, France, Italy, and Sweden, which were ahead of the United States in the use of industrial robots. This allows them to obtain an estimate of the global technology advances available to US producers prior to widespread US adoption, and thus not influenced by idiosyncratic US factors. They use Community Business Patterns data for 1980 (which was prior to the introduction of industrial robots) to obtain data on employment patterns across US commuting zones, allowing them to estimate the change in exposure to industrial robots based on analogous European industries. We crosswalk these values calculated at the commuting zone to the county level.

exposed to automation and thus throw their support behind Trump in 2016 (Frey, Berger, and Chen 2018).

Column 9 is a regression estimated via IV that is identical to Column 8, Table 1, except that it includes Automation Risk, an estimate of the percentage of jobs at the county level that could be automated in 2015. This measure is based on 2015 data on county-level industry employment, drawing from the American Community Survey, together with estimates of the percentage of automatable jobs within different industries from Muro et al. (2019).[88] Column 9 reveals that when controlling for Automation Risk, however, the coefficient on log(Patents Per Capita) is −2.47 (p-value < 0.001), compared to −2.566 in Model 8 (Table 1).

Column 10 is a model that simultaneously includes all the potential alternative channels by which our demographic, geographic, and climatic instruments may influence electoral support for Trump in 2016 that we outlined earlier. We return to using Robot Exposure instrumented with Robot Exposure European Analogs. Like Column 8, Table 1, this specification also includes state-fixed effects and the numerous additional variables included in that specification: the Autor et al. (2020) China Shock variable instrumented with the initial shares of employment in a given location and industry multiplied by the growth of Chinese imports in eight developed countries during the same time window, their suite of controls, and the additional control variables we introduced, including log(Real Median Income Per Capita), the Unemployment Rate, and the Rurality Index.

Column 10 reveals that despite including all of these additional variables, the coefficient on log(Patents Per Capita) is −2.221 (p-value = 0.01), compared to −2.566 in Model 8 (Table 1). These results are almost identical to our baseline, bivariate instrument specification results in column 2b, Table 1, where the coefficient for patents per capita is −2.219 (p-value = 0.001).

7.4 Robustness to Innovation Measure and Trumpism Measure

Are our results robust to how we measure innovation? Table 5, Columns 1 to 3, includes several robustness tests to find out using an IV estimation strategy and specification reported in Table 1, Column 8: that is, including the same instrumental variables in the first-stage regression, the shift-share instrument for

---

[88] The American Community Survey provides estimates for the county-level employment across NAICS industry categories in 2015, which we multiply by the percentage of jobs at risk of automation according to Muro et al. (2019). This allows us to create an average of the number of jobs at risk in a given county based on their employment across different industries. To create Automation Risk, we calculate the average percentage of jobs at risk across all industries at the county level.

Table 5 The determinants of Trumpism: Additional robustness tests

PANEL A

Dependent Variable	(1) Trump vs. Bush 2000	(2) Trump vs. Bush 2000	(3) Trump vs. Bush 2000	(4) Trump vs. Bush 2004	(5) Trump vs. McCain 2008
Patent Measurement	Patents P.C., 2008	Patents P.C., 1990	Patents P.C., 1930	Patents P.C., 2000	Patents P.C., 2000
Sample	Full	Full	Full	Full	Full
Patents Per Capita	−2.564***	−3.253***	−5.477***	−0.018***	−0.009***
	[0.662]	[1.488]	[1.758]	[0.006]	[0.004]
China Trade Shock	2.649	−0.319	−0.226	0.016*	0.009
	[1.669]	[1.391]	[1.547]	[0.009]	[0.006]
Shift Share Instrument	Yes	Yes	Yes	Yes	Yes
State-Fixed Effects	Yes	Yes	Yes	Yes	Yes
Baseline Controls	Yes	Yes	Yes	Yes	Yes
Additional Controls	Yes	Yes	Yes	Yes	Yes
Observations	2,653	2,787	1,607	2,630	2,628

Table 5 (cont.)

PANEL B

	(6)	(7)	(8)	(9)	(10)
Dependent Variable	Trump vs. Romney 2012	Trump vs. Bush 2000	Trump vs. Bush 2000	Trump vs. Bush 2000	Trump vs. Bush 2000
Patent Measurement	Patents P.C., 2000	Patents P.C., 2000	Patents P.C., 2000	Patents P.C., 2000	Patents P.C., 2000
Sample	Full	Excluding Silicon Valley	Excluding Route 128	Excluding N.C. Res. Tri.	Excluding all big clusters
Patents Per Capita	-0.011***	-3.069***	-2.561***	-2.539***	-3.012***
	[0.004]	[0.873]	[0.643]	[0.639]	[0.869]
China Trade Shock	0.009	0.644	1.297	1.378	0.744
	[0.007]	[1.406]	[1.302]	[1.267]	[1.364]
Shift Share Instrument	Yes	Yes	Yes	Yes	Yes
State-Fixed Effects	Yes	Yes	Yes	Yes	Yes
Baseline Controls	Yes	Yes	Yes	Yes	Yes
Additional Controls	Yes	Yes	No	Yes	Yes
Observations	2,630	2,648	2,650	2,646	2,638

Notes: Significant at the 0.01 level (***); significant at the 0.05 level (**); significant at the 0.10 level (*). Following Autor et al. (2020), we calculate "Trumpism" by subtracting the two-party Republican vote share in 2000 from the two-party Republican vote share in different years. We exclude Alaska and Hawaii because of missing data. The patent per capita measures are logged. We estimate, but do not report, first-stage regression results for each of these regressions estimated via IV: the excluded instruments are Temperature, Precipitation, their interaction, and log(Population Density), all measured in 1900. We cluster the standard errors across all models by commuting zone and weigh the observations by counties' total votes in the baseline, comparing the presidential election. See text for what variables are included in both the Baseline Controls and Additional Controls.

China Trade Shock, state-fixed effects, and the same control variables. In Column 1, rather than measure the level of patents per capita in 2000, we use patents per capita in 2008.[89] Increasing patents per capita by 1 percentage point during this window leads to a decrease in Trumpism of 2.6 percentage points (p-value < 0.001). In Column 2, we measure innovation as log(Patents Per Capita) in 1990; increasing patents per capita by 1% that year leads to a decrease of 2.3 percentage points (p-value < 0.001) in the two-party vote share for Trump in 2016 versus Bush in 2000. In Column 3, we instead use log(Patents Per Capita) in 1930; increasing patents per capita by 1% leads to a decrease of 5.5 percentage points (p-value = 0.002) in Trumpism.

Are our results robust to the way we measure Trumpism? To find out, Table 5, Columns 4 to 6, includes several robustness tests using the IV estimation strategy and the specification reported in Table 1, Column 8. We now return to using log(Patents Per Capita in 2000) to measure innovation. In Column 4, rather than measure Trumpism as the two-party vote share for Trump in 2016 versus Bush in 2000, we measure it as the vote share for Trump versus Bush in 2004.[90] In Column 5, we measure it as the vote share for Trump versus McCain in 2008; in Column 6, as the vote share for Trump versus Romney in 2012. The results of these experiments confirm our main results: more innovation is statistically significantly related to less support for Trumpism, no matter how we measure the latter.

7.5 Robustness to Excluding Major Innovation Clusters

Are our results robust to excluding major innovation clusters such as Silicon Valley? To find out, we return to measuring Trumpism as the two-party vote share for Trump in 2016 versus Bush in 2000 and continue to measure innovation as log(Patents Per Capita in 2000). We also continue to use the IV framework and specification reported in Table 1, Column 8. The only difference is that, in Table 5, Columns 7 to 10, we experiment with excluding different innovation clusters that may have exercised an outsized effect on our results hitherto from the estimation.

These geographically censored models are as follows. In Column 7, we exclude the Silicon Valley counties from the regression (Santa Clara, San Mateo, San Francisco, Alameda, and Contra Costa). In Column 8, we exclude the Route 128 counties (Norfolk, Middlesex, and Essex). In Column 9, we exclude the North Carolina Research Triangle counties (Durham, Chatham,

---

[89] While the minimum value for this variable is −100, the mean is −19.7, the maximum is 1,594, and the standard deviation is 77.6.

[90] We weigh the regression by the counties' total votes in the 2004 presidential election; for the following regressions, we adjust the weights accordingly as our baseline changes; for example, in Column 5, we weigh the regression by the counties' total votes in the 2008 presidential election.

Franklin, Vance, Wake, Orange, and Wilson). In Column 10, we exclude all of the counties that belong to these major innovation clusters simultaneously; that is, we drop Silicon Valley, Route 128, and the North Carolina Research Triangle from the regression.

Across each of these experiments, log(Patents Per Capita) remains strongly negative associated with Trumpism, both statistically and substantively. We surmise that American voters in innovative places rejected Trump in the 2016 presidential election across the country, even outside of major technological hubs.

7.6 Taking Stock of the Empirical Results

This section suggests that our Element's main finding, that more innovative counties are negatively associated with Trumpism in 2016, is both causal and resilient. It is robust to an IV approach that exploits the exogenous sources of spatial variation in innovation outlined in Section 6. It also holds once we control for localized China Trade Shocks after China joined the WTO in 2001, as well as instrumenting those shocks with a shift-share measure of trade exposure, as Autor et al. (2020) do. It is robust to state-fixed effects, a host of other control variables, including demographic variables, living standards, unemployment rates, educational levels, and how rural the county is, as well as corrections for spatial correlation.

Perhaps most importantly, it is also robust to several diagnostics that relax the exclusion restriction (assume that the instruments may have a direct effect on Trumpism) and holds after accounting for alternative channels by which our demographic, geographic, and climatic instrumental variables may affect electoral support for Trump in 2016. These include measures of population density today, evangelical adherence per capita, college density, student enrollment in higher education, attitudes about climate change, exposure to industrial robots, and automation risk. As in the case of localized China Trade Shocks, we instrument robot exposure with a shift-share exogenous measure of robot exposure, as Frey, Berger, and Chen (2018) do.

Additionally, the regression results hold if we measure the main variables differently. First, if we change how we operationalize innovation: either as the change in patents per capita between 2000 and 2008, patents per capita in 1990, or patents per capita in 1930. Second, if we compare Trump's 2016 electoral percentage versus the share earned by other GOP presidential candidates other than George W. Bush in prior election years.

Finally, the finding that more innovation maps onto less support for Trumpism is robust to whether we relegate attention to counties outside of America's most prominent innovation clusters.

In short, the regression results we report in this section show that Trump did significantly worse electorally in more innovative places. We submit this is a causal relationship. We suggest that this pattern was driven by the economic interests of residents of innovation clusters that clashed with Trump's economic agenda.

We now turn to investigating the policies Trump adopted after he assumed the presidency and their effect on the economic wellbeing of US innovation clusters. We then evaluate what impact this had on his electoral prospects in the 2020 presidential election.

8 Innovation, President Trump, and the 2020 Elections

In this section, we document President Trump's track record on innovation and look at the political consequences of his policies. First, we outline his record on immigration, education, infrastructure, R&D, basic science, and other issues bearing on US technological development; we also analyze their impact on innovation and the negative reaction they engendered in the high-tech community. Second, we emulate the econometric framework introduced in the previous section: we systematically evaluate the relationship between innovation and Trumpism at the county level in the 2020 presidential election. We now measure Trumpism as Trump's presidential vote share in 2020 versus Bush's. Third, we ask: did Trump's presidency further move the political needle against him among counties that were relatively more innovative? We alternatively capture Trumpism as the difference between Trump's 2020 and 2016 vote shares. We then evaluate whether changes in patenting between 2016 and 2020 map onto changes between presidential elections in both electoral support for Trump and financial contributions to his campaigns.

This section's rich qualitative and quantitative evidence confirms that, during his presidency, Trump followed through with the unique brand of populism he espoused during the 2016 presidential campaign. He delivered on his bid to "make America great again" by enacting trade protectionism, pursuing and threatening antitrust lawsuits against big tech firms and similar punitive measures, including flirting with rescinding Section 230 of the Communications Decency Act, and otherwise foregoing making public investments that drive innovation. Trump also took tangible steps to reduce immigration by skilled foreign workers who are usually hired by innovative firms to help them remain globally competitive. His protectionism undermined the global supply chains and technology transfer networks relied upon by innovative US firms.[91]

---

[91] While on the campaign trail, Candidate Biden spoke in favor of privacy protections and personal data standards like those adopted by the EU through the General Data Protection Regulation (GDPR) framework by giving consumers stronger property rights over their data, including restrictions on how digital platforms use it, the reporting of security breaches, and

We find, akin to the previous section, that innovation is negatively associated with the 2020 version of Trumpism. This suggests that US citizens living close to innovative companies had not fully priced in Trump's negative effect on their local industries in 2016; it took his actual presidency to further alienate them politically. And this seemed to matter: the erosion of electoral support for Trumpism in innovation clusters in battleground states such as Arizona and Georgia, which had gone for Trump in 2016, contributed to him losing the presidency in 2020.

8.1 Trumpism in 2020

Figure 13 displays the unweighted county-level change in the two-party vote share received by the Republican presidential candidate between the 2000 and 2020 elections. As in the 2016 presidential election, locations differed substantially in their reaction to Trump. For the 2,256 counties with data, the variable's mean value is a 6.98 swing (change in percentage of the two-party vote obtained by Trump versus Bush in 2000).[92]

There is again, as in 2016, considerable heterogeneity within states in support for Trumpism in 2020. Notable examples include Texas, Washington, Florida, Colorado, and Utah. The 2020 presidential election results also show that Trumpism was relatively popular in red states that voted Republican in 2000. This includes Texas and Louisiana, for example, where Trump improved over Bush's 2000 vote totals by 8.73 and 10 percentage points, respectively. Conversely, Trump registered strong electoral gains in the Appalachian and Midwest regions, especially the Rust Belt, vis-à-vis Bush; the average value for Trumpism in Michigan, Wisconsin, Pennsylvania, and Ohio in 2020 is 8.33 (percentage point improvement over Bush in 2000), and the median is 7.53.

However, since Trump lost the presidency in 2020, he underperformed in relation to his showing in 2016; Figure 14 helps us understand the geography of

---

a right to be "forgotten." President Trump, conversely, did not seem supportive of these ideas (see Finch et al. 2020). As president, Biden pushed through the reestablishment of so-called Net Neutrality, which had been rescinded under Trump's watch, thereby barring content providers from engaging in price discrimination by charging some websites more for faster internet speeds. His administration was also much more aggressive in pursuing antitrust suits against Big Tech.

[92] The standard deviation is 10.8; the minimum value is −27.0; and the maximum value is 48.9. As was the case when evaluating Trumpism in 2016, a histogram of the distribution of Trumpism in 2020, juxtaposed with a normal distribution (not shown), reveals that the data resembles a bell curve. This is attested to by the fact that the mean and median are essentially identical: 7 and 7.4, respectively. If we weigh by a county's total votes in 2000, which we do in the regressions that follow, per Autor et al. (2020), the mean change between 2000 and 2020 is −1.58 and the standard deviation is 9.93. We note that the MIT Election Data and Science Lab had not yet reported observations for some states when we conducted this analysis, reducing our data coverage versus the 2016 elections (see Section 7).

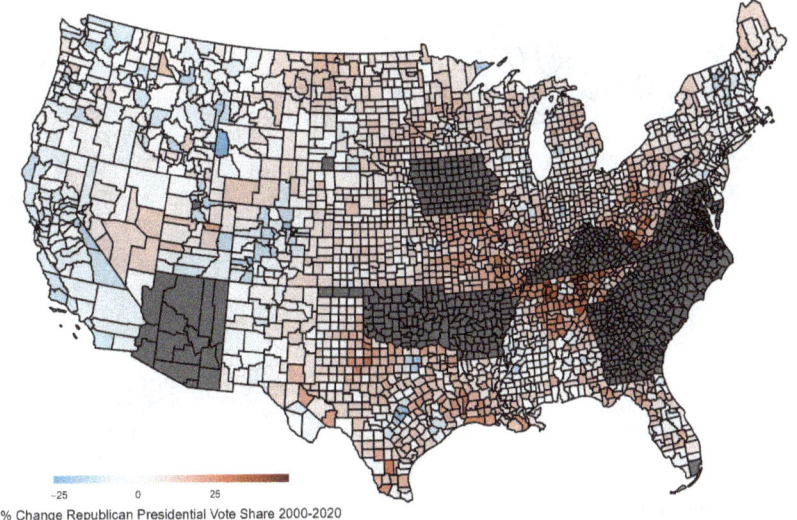

Figure 13 Electoral support for Trumpism in 2020 across the Continental United States

Note: Inspired by Autor et al. (2020), we calculate "Trumpism" by subtracting the two-party Republican vote share in 2000 from the two-party Republican vote share in 2020. Like they do, we exclude Alaska and Hawaii because of missing data. Unlike for the 2016 presidential elections, other states are missing data because it had not yet been reported as of the time of this analysis.
Source: MIT Election Data and Science Lab.

his electoral loss. It graphs the difference between Trump's 2020 vote percentage (as a share of the two-party vote) versus Trump's 2016 vote percentage on a county-by-county basis. The average change in his county vote share is −0.66 percentage points (the median is −0.78), and the standard deviation is 2.63.

While the overall story behind these numbers is complex, two major patterns stand out. First, Trump lost considerable support in 2020 in places he managed to peel away from the Democrats in 2016. Second, Trump lost the support of innovation clusters in battleground states, which may have ultimately cost him the presidency.

In Michigan, Ohio, Pennsylvania, and Wisconsin, Trump received 0.57 percentage points fewer votes in 2020 versus 2016. And, in states with similar industrial profiles to that region, Trump also underperformed: for example, the change in his vote share in Minnesota was −1.4 percentage points; in Illinois, it was −0.04.

Therefore, to help win the presidency in 2020, Biden banked votes from white working-class men, many of whom had supported Trump in 2016

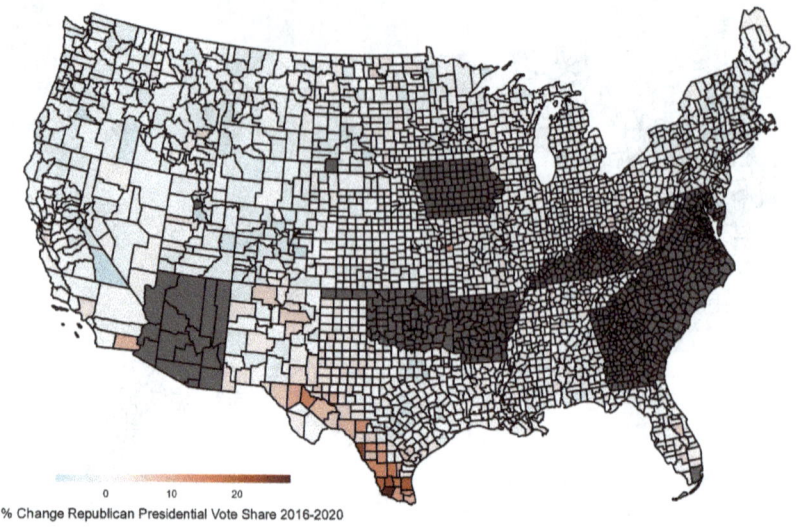

Figure 14 Electoral support for Trumpism in 2020 versus 2016

Note: To obtain this measure we subtract the two-party Republican vote share in 2016 from the two-party Republican vote share in 2020. As before, we exclude Alaska and Hawaii. Unlike for the 2016 presidential elections, other states are missing data because it had not yet been reported as of the time of this analysis.
Source: MIT Election Data and Science Lab.

(see Williams 2020). While Trump was victorious in Ohio, and overwhelmingly won rural districts across the Midwest, Biden won with strong support in the major cities across these states. This includes Detroit, Michigan, Milwaukee, Wisconsin, and Akron, Ohio. Moreover, if we consider the Rust Belt to include cities such as Buffalo, NY; Corning, NY; Rochester, NY; Utica, NY; East Lansing, MI; and Flint, MI, Joe Biden also beat Trump in those places.

A deeper look at the numbers confirms this picture. An election postmortem report authored by Republican pollsters affiliated with the Trump campaign in the aftermath of the 2020 presidential race evinces that the former president bled support in the Rust Belt (Fabrizio, Lee & Associates 2020).[93] The report concludes that Trump suffered great losses among demographics overrepresented in the low-skilled subgroup; he experienced sizable erosion in support among white men across every age group, including males of prime working age and those entering retirement age, two groups usually associated with unskilled workers. In the five states in which Biden beat Trump in 2020 after Trump won

---

[93] These pollsters conducted an analysis of exit polling in several battleground states, many of them located in America's industrial heartland. They include Michigan, Wisconsin, Ohio, and Pennsylvania.

in 2016, Trump's most dramatic loss of support among these voters was in the 18 to 29 age group and the 65 and older group. This suggests that, while in office, Trump's populism may have failed to persuade these voters in 2020, notwithstanding the fact that his promise to "make America great again" may have won them over in 2016.

The question now is whether this pattern, combined with further erosion of electoral support in innovative clusters in battleground states, could have cost Trump the 2020 election. Two examples of states that Trump carried in 2016, but lost in 2020, suggest that this may indeed have been the case. They are Arizona and Georgia.

First, take Arizona's so-called Easy Valley Corridor, home to a cluster of high-tech companies that has recently emerged along the Loop 101 beltway connecting Phoenix to several of its suburbs. It hosts established big tech firms such as Apple, Google, and Amazon, as well as several start-ups. In 2020, Trump lost Maricopa County, where this innovation cluster is situated, by almost 45,000 votes. He had previously beat Hillary Clinton there, in 2016, 747,361 to 702,907 votes. Maricopa is Arizona's most populous county and, therefore, Trump's loss sealed his defeat in the Grand Canyon State the second time around. While he lost Arizona to Biden by a bit more than 10,000 votes in 2020, his victory in Maricopa County in 2016 helped put him over the top statewide during that election, when he won Arizona by over 91,000 votes.

Second, consider Georgia's High Tech I-85 Corridor in the northeast part of the Peach State. It includes the greater Atlanta metro area and beyond, encompassing the following counties: Fulton, Cherokee, Cobb, Forsyth, and Gwinnett, along with the north central section of Hall County. In both Gwinnett and Cobb Counties, Biden increased his share of the vote vis-à-vis Hillary Clinton by 12 percentage points. In Cherokee County, Trump also lost 12 percentage points versus his showing in 2016; in Forsyth County, it was 16 percentage points.

We now proceed to examine whether Trump's antipathy toward innovation may have helped cost him the 2020 election nationally. We first look at how his presidency affected innovation and how some influential members of the tech community reacted to Trump's policies around immigration, trade, antitrust, and public investment.

8.2 Trump's Populist Presidency

Soon after taking office, President-elect Trump struck a conciliatory tone toward the leaders of innovative American companies, many of whom he had butted heads with during the 2016 presidential campaign. These companies were situated in dense, diverse cities centered on high-tech that had definitively preferred Hillary Clinton. For example, San Francisco voters favored Candidate Clinton by almost 85% and Seattle voters by 87%; the wider Silicon Valley went for her by over 70% (O'Mara 2022). During a December 2016 meeting with the CEO's of major high-tech firms dubbed the "Trump tech summit," which included the leaders of Facebook, Amazon, IBM, Apple, and Microsoft, he declared that "I am here to help you folks do well", and sought to mend bridges and encourage cooperation between his administration and their companies (O'Mara 2022).

Superficially, Trump seemed to champion American innovation early in his tenure, or at least railed against the putative theft of US technology by Chinese firms in a manner that was ostensibly aligned with the interests of America's high-tech companies. Right out of the gate, his administration accused both the Chinese Communist Party and Chinese firms of engaging in widespread industrial espionage; compelling American firms to enter joint ventures that divulge trade secrets in exchange for market access; conducting onerous security reviews and testing requirements; and deploying trillions of dollars to acquire US companies operating in high-tech industries (see Menaldo and Wittstock 2021).

But these seemingly pro high-tech gestures were not well received by his intended audience–and coupled with policies perceived by several innovative companies as harmful to their workforces, industries, and supply chains, triggered an early backlash against President Trump by the high-tech community (Lapowsky 2018). On January 27, 2017, he issued an executive order banning travel from several majority-Muslim countries that sparked an immediate rebuke by prominent cutting-edge firms. For example, Apple CEO Tim Cook declared that "Apple would not exist without immigration, let alone thrive and innovate the way we do" (O'Mara 2022; Swisher and Fried 2017). Google CEO Sundar Pichai, Facebook CEO Mark Zuckerberg, and other leaders of innovative US firms, also publicly denounced Trump's travel ban, noting the negative effects on American technological development, including the possibility that it might precipitate a brain drain (see O'Mara 2022; Romm 2017).

This was only the beginning. The Trump administration also halted the so-called International Entrepreneur Rule, which had made it easier for noncitizen entrepreneurs to start businesses in the United States and issued a record number of "requests for evidence" to highly skilled H-1B visa holders, making it harder for US employers to hire these immigrants (Lapowsky 2018). Moreover, early in his administration, Trump neglected to staff the Office of Science and Technology Policy (OSTP), which suffered from important vacancies, including to its director. While it took the president two years to name an OSTP director, who also serves as a US president's de facto science and technology advisor, the agency shrunk from 135 personnel to 45 during Trump's tenure.

As widely expected, Trump's presidency saw an unprecedented increase in US trade protectionism and a deterioration in globalization.[94] He introduced a host of tariff and nontariff barriers and restrictions on certain exports.[95] In particular, Trump slapped major tariffs on Chinese goods – the Trump administration increased tariffs by 25% of the 2017 value of China's imports, which was equivalent to taxing $370 billion worth of Chinese goods.[96] Beijing then imposed tit-for-tat tariffs on US exports and increased regulations on American firms doing business in China; for example, Chinese antitrust authorities' nixed Qualcomm's attempt to merge with Dutch chipmaker NXP in 2018. Trump also renegotiated NAFTA after taking power and squelched the TPP.

These policies hurt American innovation. Trump's tariffs on Chinese imports and China's retaliatory tariffs significantly raised the costs of doing business for American firms, especially high-tech ones (Menaldo and Wittstock 2021). Several measures in the renegotiated NAFTA, christened the United States-Mexico-Canada Agreement, weakened IP protections. Walking away from the TPP foreclosed new export markets for cutting-edge US firms.

Also, as foreshadowed during his 2016 presidential campaign, Trump weakened global supply chains in ways that harmed American high-tech companies.[97] His administration's actions against Huawei are emblematic. Trump supported the development of a so-called open architecture system for 5G centered on cloud computing and software that can bypass foreign equipment such as Huawei-made switches and routers. This followed on the heels of the Federal Communications Commission (FTC) labeling both China's ZTE Corporation and Huawei national

---

[94] A bipartisan consensus underpinned a US-led rules-based system after World War II, starting with the 1948 General Agreement on Tariffs and Trade (GATT) and capstoned by the 1995 World Trade Organization's (WTO) binding dispute settlement system. Irwin (2017) argues that the United States has used tariffs and the threat of tariffs since the 1934 Reciprocal Trade Agreements Act to ply, if not threaten, foreign governments into reciprocal trade liberalization.

[95] Between 1990 and 2017, the trade-weighted average global tariff applied under WTO rules fell by 4.2 percentage points. The drop was greatest in poorer countries: in the same period China's tariffs fell by 28 points, India's by 51, and Brazil's by 10. Bilateral and regional trade deals expanded from around 50 in the early 1990s to as many as 300 in 2019. These have cut trade weighted applied tariffs by a further 2.3 percentage points. This system supported an explosion of global trade as a share of gross output, from around 30% in the early 1970s to 60% in the early 2010s. Over the same period complex global supply chains grew from around 37% to 50% of total trade (see The Economist 2021: 3).

[96] The Trump administration also imposed import tariffs on steel and aluminum, solar panels, and an assortment of European goods.

[97] This also included Trump's efforts to block some mergers and acquisitions. For example, his administration prevented Canyon Bridge Capital Partners from acquiring Lattice Semiconductor Corporation, alleging the deal would have been financed by Chinese money.

security threats, banning ZTE and Huawei from providing equipment to America's wireless communications network, and ending their federal subsidies. The Trump administration also heavily restricted semiconductor firms from selling microchips and software to Huawei, ZTE, and other Chinese firms, at first forcing the former to obtain a license and, eventually, banning some of them from doing so outright. Trump banned Huawei from America's 5G network entirely and prevented the American government and US telecommunication companies from procuring and using the company's products.[98]

Though Trump's professed reason for more restrictive trade, FDI, and technology policies vis-à-vis China was to protect American national security, US semiconductor industry trade groups strongly complained about the potential loss of profits and jobs associated with his administration's restrictions on microchip and software exports.[99] A 2020 report by the Boston Consulting Group, commissioned by the US Semiconductor Industry Association, concludes that the Trump administration's policies undermine the competitive position of American chip companies, reducing their market shares, revenues, and employment (Varas and Varadarajan 2020). American companies like Qualcomm, Broadcom, Micron, Intel, Microsoft, IBM, and Google benefitted substantially from providing Chinese companies with everything from microchips and software to consulting services; that is, until the Trump administration implemented license requirements to sell chips to Chinese companies.[100] This includes royalty revenues generated by IP licenses. Until a similar 2019 ban, several US tech firms also earned a pretty penny exporting computer chips and related technologies to the Chinese government to help it power its supercomputer industry.

American companies beyond semiconductors, including some involved in AI (such as Google) and biotechnology, also objected to Chinese export bans and similar trade and capital restrictions.[101] They were worried about losing access to China's lucrative market.[102] They were also concerned about weakening

---

[98] To be sure, on the campaign trail during the 2020 presidential election, Candidate Biden largely agreed with Trump's circumspection toward foreign-made telecommunications equipment making its way into the 5G network. See Finch et al. (2020).

[99] China is the biggest market for American semiconductors, typically purchasing about 25% of US chips (amounting to hundreds of billions of dollars in sales).

[100] Indeed, Intel, Qualcomm, and other American chipmakers quietly pushed back against the US government's ban on exports to Huawei, lobbying the Commerce Department to rescind them. See Nellis et al. (2019).

[101] In 2018, the US government passed the Foreign Investment Risk Review Modernization Act; it was (at least) partly intended to reduce Chinese FDI in areas that are deemed sensitive to US national security.

[102] For example, in the first quarter of 2020, the Chinese market made up 20% of Apple's total sales and almost 15% of its total revenue.

transnational R&D networks that connect American and Chinese firms, research institutes, and universities (Menaldo and Wittstock 2021). In this vein, Trump constantly scolded Apple, especially on Twitter, hectoring them to make their iPhone in the United States to avoid the increased costs of doing business borne by his Chinese import tariffs.[103] After much lobbying by Apple CEO Tim Cook, Trump ultimately agreed to exempt Apple from announced tariffs on laptops and smartphones imported from China (O'Mara 2022). A snake-bitten Apple nevertheless invested in rerouting some of its manufacturing supply chain to Korea and Vietnam.[104]

Trump also took the fight to other big tech firms. He pushed the Justice Department to sue Time Warner and AT&T to prevent their vertical merger.[105] As president, he continued his 2016 presidential campaign habit of badmouthing and threatening digital platforms and their leaders. For example, he repeatedly locked horns with Amazon's Jeff Bezos, over both his ownership of *The Washington Post* and Amazon's tax bill. Trump also directed the US Post Office (USPO) to investigate whether its delivery of Amazon packages was harming it even though Amazon's delivery orders had boosted USPO's business. He continued to single out and threaten other digital platforms such as Facebook, Google, and Twitter, often accusing them of peddling fake news and censoring conservative views.

Railing against "special protections" for digital platforms, Trump repeatedly called on the Federal Communications Commission (FCC) to rescind Section 230.[106] While Candidate Biden agreed with Trump during the 2020 presidential campaign on this, he also stressed self-policing as a better solution for improving content moderation (see Finch et al. 2020) and shied away from doing so after becoming president. President Trump's numerous attacks on the press were also often directed toward social media companies and search engines, especially Facebook, Twitter, and Google, which he accused of "anti-conservative bias" and of being in covert alliance with the Democratic Party (O'Mara 2022).[107]

---

[103] Only one of several examples is this Trump tweet: "Apple prices may increase because of the massive tariffs we may be imposing on china but there is an easy solution where there would be zero tax and indeed a tax incentive make your products in the united states instead of china start building new plants now. Exciting!" TTA– Search (thetrumparchive.com).

[104] Cook also visited an Apple contractor in Texas together with President Trump, who touted the reshoring of jobs to the United States (O'Mara 2022).

[105] The federal government lost the suit in court under President Trump's Justice Department.

[106] Section 230 is the lifeblood of the internet as we know it, in that it immunizes digital platforms from liability for the content posted by third party users. This reduces their exposure to lawsuits, allowing them to reach global scale economies and monetize user data. See Finch et al. (2020).

[107] Under the Trump administration, the (FTC) launched probes into Facebook and the Justice Department sued Google on antitrust grounds. During his presidency, both parties converged on the idea of strengthening competition in the digital space by "cracking down" on big tech (see Finch et al. 2020).

Over his presidency, while Trump's budgets modestly increased funding for research in some targeted technology areas, especially AI and 5G, they sought overall cuts for basic research, R&D in cutting-edge areas, and education (Atkinson et al. 2020).[108] This included plans to slash budgets for the National Institutes of Health (NIH), the National Science Foundation (NSF), and R&D programs run by the DOE and the National Aeronautics and Space Administration (NASA). His administration cut funding for clean energy R&D and eliminated federal programs and tax incentives for clean energy development (Finch et al. 2020). Trump cut funding for the Advanced Research Projects Agency-Energy (ARPA-E), which George W. Bush had signed into law during his presidency. He also pushed for reductions in funding for so-called STEM (Science, Technology, Engineering, and Math) education while bolstering support for apprenticeship programs (Atkinson et al. 2020; Mervis 2018).

President Trump's policies not only worsened the already fraught relationship he had with the high-tech industry since the 2016 presidential elections, but they cast a shadow on his 2020 reelection bid.[109] So much so that several computer industry luminaries, including the vast majority of living Turing Award winners, departed from their typically apolitical stance and endorsed Biden over Trump during the 2020 presidential election. They declared jointly in a signed letter that

> Computer Science is at its best when its learnings and discoveries are shared freely in the spirit of progress. These core values helped make America a leader in information technology, so vital in this Information Age. Joe Biden and Kamala Harris listen to experts before setting public policy, essential when science and technology may help with many problems facing our nation today.[110]

8.3 Econometric Strategy

As we did in the previous section, we now evaluate the systematic, spatial relationship between innovation and Trumpism. However, we now do so for

---

[108] Trump floated the idea that the Defense Department should create a 5G network that is then leased to private network providers at different points throughout his presidency, but no telecommunications companies seemed interested in this proposal (see Finch et al. 2020).

[109] Two exceptions to this general trend may include his administration's reduction in corporate tax rates and its endorsement of flexible labor practices in relation to the gig economy, specifically, the Labor Department's decision under his presidency to continue to label workers who participate in these markets as independent contractors instead of employees, which Candidate Biden opposed during the 2020 election. See Finch et al. (2020).

[110] The Turing Award is widely considered the "Nobel Prize in computing" and the recipients include leading architects of the semiconductor industry, the internet, and AI. As of 2020, there were thirty-five still living people who had received the award. See https://int.nyt.com/data/documenttools/the-statement-from-the-turing-award-winners-on-their-biden-endorsement/c0b01c987a946137/full.pdf.

2020 instead of 2016. Like Section 7, we start simply. Table 6, Column 1, reports the bivariate relationship between log(Patents Per Capita, in 2000) and Trumpism estimated via OLS, where we now measure the latter as the difference in the two-party vote share earned by Trump in 2020 versus Bush in 2000. Increasing per capita patents by 1% maps onto a decrease in Trumpism of 1.36 (p-value < 0.001), which is stronger than the negative relationship reported in Section 7, where increasing Per Capita Patents by 1% increases the 2016 version of Trumpism by 1.19 percentage points (p-value < 0.001). Moreover, the r-squared for the 2020 version of the model is 0.16; it is 0.15 for its 2016 counterpart.

To ascertain whether this relationship is causal, as we submit it is for the relationship between innovation and Trumpism in 2016 reported in Section 7, we return to the strategy we pursued there, and estimate IV models conducted in two stages. The first again estimates the determinants of log(Per Capita Patents) using excluded instruments. The second stage again estimates the determinants of Trumpism, but this time the 2020 version. We again follow Autor et al. (2020), and both cluster the standard errors by commuting zone (addressing the spatial correlation between counties in encompassing metro areas) and weigh the observations by counties' total votes in the 2000 presidential election. For the second-stage regression, the most important thing to note is once again whether the predicted values of per capita patents calculated from the first-stage regression explain the variation in Trumpism.

As in Section 7, the first-stage regression of our IV regression with controls is:

$$w_i = \alpha_j + \beta X_i + \xi(\phi_i + \lambda_i + \phi_i \times \lambda_i) + \pi(\psi_i) + u_i \tag{4}$$

in which w_i is the estimated value of log(Patents per Capita) for county i; α_j identifies invariant state-fixed effects potentially correlated with X, a vector of k explanatory variables in 2000 associated with β estimated parameters; ξ are estimates associated with ϕ_i, county Temperature in 1900, λ_i, county Precipitation in 1900, and their interaction; π are estimates of ψ_i, county Population Density in 1900 (in logs); and u_i is an error term.

The second stage of the regression is:

$$y_i = \alpha_j + \beta X_i + u_i \tag{5}$$

in which y_i is the estimated value of Trumpism for county i; (first measured as the difference in vote share for Trump in 2020 versus Bush in 2000; then as the difference in vote share for Trump in 2020 versus his vote share in 2016); α_j addresses invariant state-fixed effects potentially correlated with X, a vector of k explanatory variables that include the predicted values of patents per capita produced by equation (4); β are estimated parameters; and u_i is an error term.

Table 6 The determinants of Trumpism in 2020

PANEL A

	(1)	(2)	(3)	(4)	(5)
Dependent Variable	2020 Trumpism	2020 Trumpism	2020 Trumpism	2020 Trumpism	2020 Trumpism
Estimation Strategy	OLS	IV (Stage 2)	IV (Stage 2)	IV (Stage 2)	IV (Stage 2)
log(Patents Per Capita)	−1.349***	−1.283*	−1.602**	−1.565**	−4.845***
	[0.089]	[0.698]	[0.744]	[0.789]	[0.866]
China Trade Shock			2.625***	3.394**	4.487***
			[0.089]	[1.520]	[1.136]
Shift Share Instrument	No	No	No	Yes	Yes
State-Fixed Effects	No	No	No	No	Yes
Baseline Controls	No	No	No	No	No
Additional Controls	No	No	No	No	No
Observations	2,114	1,962	1,962	1,969	1,962

PANEL B

	(5)	(7)	(8)	(9)	(10)
Dependent Variable	2020 Trumpism	2020 Trumpism	2020 Trumpism	Trump '20-Trump '16	Trump '20-Trump '16
Estimation Strategy	IV (Stage 2)	IV (Stage 2)	IV (Stage 2)	OLS	OLS
Innovation Measure;	P.C. Patents, 2000	P.C. Patents, 2000	P.C. Patents, 2000	Patents '20-Patents '16	Patents '20-Patents '16
	−1.974***	−2.309***	−4.689**	−0.011***	−9495.138***
	[0.754]	[0.725]	[2.175]	[0.004]	[2397.092]

China Trade Shock	2.633	2.611	3.438	0.058	−321873.3***
	[1.650]	[1.659]	[2.373]	[0.112]	[34961.64]
Shift Share Instrument	Yes	Yes	Yes	No	No
State-Fixed Effects	Yes	Yes	Yes	Yes	Yes
Baseline Controls	Yes	Yes	Yes	Yes	Yes
Additional Controls	No	Yes	Yes	Yes	Yes
Observations	1,962	1,957	1,957	2,246	3,092

Notes: Significant at the 0.01 level (***); significant at the 0.05 level (**); significant at the 0.10 level (*). Inspired by Autor et al. (2020), we calculate "Trumpism" by subtracting the two-party Republican vote share in 2000 from the two-party Republican vote share in 2020 across most models. In Column 9, we instead look at the difference between Trump's percent of the vote share in 2020 versus 2016. In Column 10, the dependent variable is the difference in Trump's campaign contributions in 2020 versus 2016 expressed in real 2020 dollars. We estimate, but do not report, first-stage regression results for the regressions estimated via IV in which the excluded instruments are Temperature, Precipitation, their interaction, and log(Population Density), all measured in 1900. We cluster the standard errors across all models by commuting zone.

As we did in Section 7, prior to estimating the model in Table 6, Column 7, we discuss simpler models. We relegate attention to the second stage regressions estimated via IV; in other words, equation (5).[111] As before, we proceed from the simplest to most complex models.

8.4 Simple to Complex Regression Approach

Let us first consider Columns 2 to 4. In Column 2, the only variable is log(Per Capita Patents). Innovation leads to less Trumpism: increasing log(Patents Per Capita) by 1% decreases Trump's share of the 2020 two-party presidential vote by 1.3 percentage points vis-à-vis Bush's vote share in 2000 (p-value = 0.07). The r-squared is 0.17. In Column 3, as we did in Section 7, when Trumpism is measured as the difference between Trump's vote share in 2016 and Bush's in 2000, we add China Trade Shock. Our results strengthen: log(Patents Per Capita) is now statistically significant at the 97% level and has a stronger magnitude. In Column 4, we instrument China Trade Shock with the Autor et al. (2020) shift-share instrument (see Section 7); the effect of log(Patents Per Capita) on Trumpism is materially unchanged.

Columns 5 to 8 perform more robustness tests. In Column 5, we introduce state-fixed effects. Our results experience a three-fold rise in magnitude (increasing patents per capita by 1% engenders a 4.5 percentage point decrease in the Republican two-party vote share in 2020 versus 2000; p-value < 0.001). In Column 6, we add the same baseline controls as in Table 1, Column 7, when we evaluated the relationship between innovation and Trumpism in 2016.[112] While the substantive effect of patents per capita weakens, it is still statistically significant at the highest possible level. Column 7 introduces additional controls, beyond the baseline ones.[113] The substantive and statistical significance of our results strengthens.[114] Column 8 reports the regression results from an LIML estimator, a linear combination of OLS and IV estimates, with the weights (approximately) eliminating any bias introduced by a regression run

---

[111] We estimate, but do not report, the first stage regression results across our models where we instrument log(Patents Per Capita) with Temperature, Precipitation and Population Density, all measured in 1900. For those results, see Table 1, Column 2a.

[112] As in the previous section, they include employment in the manufacturing sector; the share of occupations that involve routinized work; the share of occupations that can be outsourced overseas; census division dummies; demographic controls that measure the share of the population across different age groups, races, gender, education levels, and immigration status; and election controls that measure the Republican two-party vote share in the 1992 and 1996 presidential elections.

[113] We add log(Real Median Income Per Capita); Unemployment Rate; and Waldorf and Kim's (2015) Rurality Index. See Section 7 for a more in-depth discussion.

[114] The results are even stronger if we use patents per capita in 2015 instead of 2000 and materially similar if we use patents per capita in 2020.

with weak instruments (see Hahn and Hausman 2003); the model is otherwise identical in terms of the variables included in Column 7. Compared to Column 7, patents per capita is considerably stronger in magnitude.

In an effort to bias against ourselves and make it very difficult to obtain a negative relationship between innovation and Trumpism in 2020, in Column 9 we measure Trumpism as the percentage of the vote share obtained by Trump in 2020 versus 2016. In terms of operationalizing innovation, we now focus on the change in the stock of patents between 2020 and 2016, which we log.[115] Because we are now focusing on change over time for both the dependent and independent variables, we switch our econometric approach to a linear regression estimated via OLS, which means we no longer instrument patents with geographic or demographic variables, nor do we instrument China Trade Shock with the shift-share instrument.[116] As in Columns 7 and 8, however, we continue to control for state-fixed effects and the full gamut of control variables.[117]

The results of this regression are as we expected: more innovation from 2016 to 2020 means less Trumpism during this period. All else equal, places that saw increases in patenting between 2016 and 2020 also saw lower voting percentages for Trump between presidential elections: increasing the stock of patents by 1% maps onto a 0.01 percentage point reduction in Trumpism (p-value < 0.001).[118] This corresponds to a one standard deviation increase in patenting inducing 3% of a standard deviation less support for Trump. We suspect that because voters had most likely priced in his populist politics by 2020, the

---

[115] When we combine the 2016 and 2020 elections in a pooled dataset and estimate a two-way fixed effects model, we obtain results consistent with the idea that more innovation means less support for Trump at the local level. This is the case for both when the outcome of interest is the share of the vote for Trump at the county level versus the vote for Bush in 2000 (Trumpism) and campaign contributions given to Trump at the county level. To arrive at this finding, we estimate Driscoll Kraay Standard Errors to address any groupwise heteroskedasticity and spatial/contemporaneous correlation and the Newey West adjustment to address serial correlation. When the dependent variable is Trumpism, we learn that an increase in patents between 2016 and 2020 of 1% translates into a reduction in electoral support for Trump between the 2016 and 2020 elections of .01 percentage point (p-value < 0.001). When the dependent variable is Campaign Contributions to Trump, we learn that an increase in patents between 2016 and 2020 of 1% translates into a reduction in campaign contributions for Trump between elections of $709.51 (p-value < 0.001). Because of several disadvantages associated with estimating a fixed effects model in levels when there are only two time periods, however, we will focus attention on the first differenced models discussed earlier.

[116] The geographic and demographic variables are county Temperature in 1900, county Precipitation in 1900, their interaction, and county Population Density in 1900 (in logs).

[117] We again cluster the standard errors by commuting zone but now weigh the regressions by the total county votes cast in the 2016 presidential election.

[118] The results are robust to controlling for the total stock of patents in 2015 to address the fact that patenting inequality between counties has decreased closer in time, which suggests that places with a higher stock of patents are less likely to experience bigger increases in patenting than places with a lower stock of patents. They are also robust to controlling for the level of Trumpism in 2016: the difference between Trump's vote share in 2016 and Bush's in 2000.

substantive effect of greater innovation between presidential elections on changes in Trump's electoral backing is relatively muted.

What if we measure Trumpism as the change in his campaign contributions between the 2016 presidential election and 2020 election? To construct this measure, we use data from the FEC on all individual campaign contributions made to Trump after he obtained the share of primary election support he needed to become the presumptive Republican presidential nominee in April 2016, until the election in November 2016. Similarly, we obtain data on the individual campaign contributions made to Trump between April 2020, when he was again crowned the presumptive Republican presidential nominee, and the election in November 2020.

To create county-level observations on the total contributions made to Trump in 2016 and in 2020, we aggregate this individual-level data to the county level.[119] We then calculate the difference in county-level campaign contributions for Trump between 2016 and 2020. Specifically, we subtract the total amount of Trump campaign donations per county in 2020 from the total amount in 2016 expressed in 2020 real dollars.

In Column 10, we report the results of this experiment: a linear regression estimated via OLS identical to Column 9, except we now measure Trumpism as the change in Trump's campaign contributions between the 2016 presidential election and the 2020 election (in 2020 real dollars). That is to say, save for this modification of the dependent variable, we continue to measure innovation as the change in the stock of patents between 2016 and 2020, introduce the same set of controls, including state-fixed effects, and cluster the standard errors similarly.[120] The results are again as we expected: increasing patents by 1% between 2016 and 2020 leads to a reduction in Trump's campaign contributions of $9,495 between 2016 and 2020 (p-value < 0.001).[121] As with the Column 9 results, where the outcome of interest is the change in electoral support for Trump between presidential elections, the magnitude of this effect is somewhat modest: a one standard deviation increase in patenting leads to 5% of a standard deviation reduction in his campaign donations.

---

[119] We aggregate total campaign contributions at the ZIP code level. We then aggregate the ZIP code totals to the county level by assigning dollar amounts to the latter according to the proportion of the ZIP code that is within the county in question, which we gleaned from the US Postal Service crosswalk.

[120] We weigh the observations by the countywide total value of campaign contributions in 2016 expressed in 2020 dollars.

[121] We also find that more patents between 2016 and 2020 map onto a reduction in the number of donors who contributed to Trump's presidential campaign in 2020 versus 2016: increasing the patent stock by 1% during this interval leads to twelve fewer Trump donors (p-value < 0.05). In the regression that yields this result, we weigh the observations by the number of donors in each county in 2016.

Taken together, these results lead us to surmise that even though Trump's populism was probably priced in by most voters and donors by 2020, innovative places may have further rejected Trump during his reelection bid. We believe that the technology-phobic policies he advanced as president had something to do with that.

8.5 The Big Picture

Like Section 7, this section again shows that our Element's main finding, that more innovation equals less Trumpism, is both causal and resilient. It holds when we measure Trumpism in 2020 versus Bush's votes in 2000, the change in Trump's vote share between 2016 and 2020, and the change in Trump's campaign contributions between presidential elections. Our results are again robust to an IV approach that exploits the exogenous sources of spatial variation in innovation outlined in Section 7. It also holds once we control for localized China Trade Shocks after China joined the WTO in 2001, as well as instrumenting those shocks with shift-share exogenous variables, as Autor et al. (2020) do. It is robust to state-fixed effects, a host of other control variables, including demographics, living standards, unemployment rates, educational levels, and how rural the county is, as well as corrections for spatial correlation.

The qualitative and quantitative evidence we report in this section strengthens our confidence that Trump's unique brand of populism hurt his electoral prospects in more innovative places across the United States. Once in office, Trump was worse for innovation than he let on during his 2016 campaign, and his antipathy toward high-tech industries may have, in some ways, cost him reelection: Trump may have sacrificed battleground states such as Arizona and Georgia to Biden. In both of those states' major innovation hubs Trump lost to the forty-sixth president in 2020, even though he had beaten Clinton there in 2016.

9 The Historical Roots of Innovation Inequality and Populism

Trump is not necessarily a new sort of populist. While we have so far shown in this Element that he has successfully capitalized on a growing socioeconomic cleavage between the economic interests of highly innovative places and those that are less oriented toward creating and commercializing new technologies, this cleavage is not new. That a political outsider like Trump would tailor populist appeals around a set of economic grievances that had been ignored hitherto by the two major parties is also not a novel phenomenon (Judis 2016; Kazin 1998). What is relatively unique about Trump, however, is that he was able to exploit innovation inequality in ways that previous populists were unable to and was elected president, in part, because of that.

In this section, we argue that American populists who *preceded* Trump indirectly also exploited geographic innovation inequality for political purposes. However, we also argue that while Trump is not different in *kind* than previous populists, he is different in *degree*: separating himself from previous populists, he elevated the political salience of innovation inequality, increasing the frequency and stridency of the appeals to less innovative places. Conversely, his policy proposals and presidency more directly antagonized innovative areas than the visions put forth by previous American populists.

Trump's ability to proffer a more modern version of populism that capitalized on differences between innovation clusters and places less integrated into globalized supply chains did not emerge out of nowhere. In this section we also document the ascendance over several decades of innovation inequality as a politically salient concern that culminated in a populist such as Trump. We explain some of the reasons behind the growing innovation gap between different places and why it became more politically combustible.

We first explore the historical political economy of American populism, focusing specifically on William Jennings Bryan and Ross Perot and culminating with Donald Trump. Both of these earlier presidential candidates were populists who previewed some of Trump's anti-innovation rhetoric and policies and, like Trump, made their appeals to less innovative places, albeit in a much more muted manner. We follow the same econometric strategy we conducted to evaluate electoral support for Trumpism in 2016 and 2020: we evaluate the causal relationship between geographic variation in innovation and electoral support for William Jennings Bryan (1900 and 1908 elections) and then for Ross Perot (1992 and 1996 elections). We find that, like those analyses, there is a negative relationship between local innovation and support for these two populists, albeit it is weaker in both magnitude and statistical significance and, for Bryan, not robust to introducing state-fixed effects. These results suggest that Trump was indeed different in degree from prior populists vis-à-vis exploiting innovation inequality, but not necessarily different in kind.

9.1 The Historical Evolution of American Innovation Inequality

We remind readers that, in Section 6, we explored the spatial persistence of American innovation inequality over time to show that places that were more innovative in the past remained more innovative in later periods. We argued that the presence of abundant biomass in some US locations with temperate climates fostered early innovation clusters during the early nineteenth century. These clusters often endured and strengthened during the ensuing decades: Places with high quantities of food and fuel attracted innovators and industrialists. These advantages were reinforced as they attracted rising levels of capital-intensive machinery, R&D activity, and talented high-skilled workers. Geographically blessed locations were therefore more likely to continue to churn out process and product innovations over succeeding industrialization waves.

However, we also remind readers that, in Section 7, we discussed R&D efforts by the federal government that often targeted places that had been less innovative prior to World War II. Washington DC's funding of science, defense contracting, and the creation of federal R&D installations created new sites of technological innovation. They spurred the creation of innovation in areas that had hitherto been innovation deserts. However, they did not necessarily translate into creating new innovation clusters akin to Silicon Valley or New England's Route 128, and any progress that federal R&D programs made in equalizing the spatial distribution of innovation proved temporary.

To put this in perspective, and to put the rest of this section in context, consider the evolution of innovation inequality in the United States across the twentieth century. Figure 15 graphs this phenomenon as the percentage of all patents granted to the top 1% of counties (those with the greatest share of patents per capita) by decade between 1920 and 2015.[122] The geographical inequality in US innovation over the long twentieth century clearly follows a U shape: inequality is very high during the beginning of the period, is then substantially reduced beginning at mid-century (as innovation became spread around more broadly, a phenomenon that reached a crescendo at the height of the Cold War), and again ramped up after 1970. In fact, it really exploded after 2000 when innovation clusters such as Silicon Valley and New England's Route 128 came to dominate the new digital economy. It reached a new apex in 2015.

Shortly ahead, we explore the reasons why innovation inequality steadily increased after 1970 and exploded during the twenty-first century, and why the political salience of this inequality has also increased over time, making Trump different in degree, but not necessarily kind, from previous populists who also exploited innovation inequality to varying degrees. Before doing that, however, it behooves us to explore the historical political economy of American populism and its complicated relationship to innovation inequality.

---

[122] When we described Figure 3 in Section 2, we explained why patents per capita is a good proxy for the spatial distribution of American innovation.

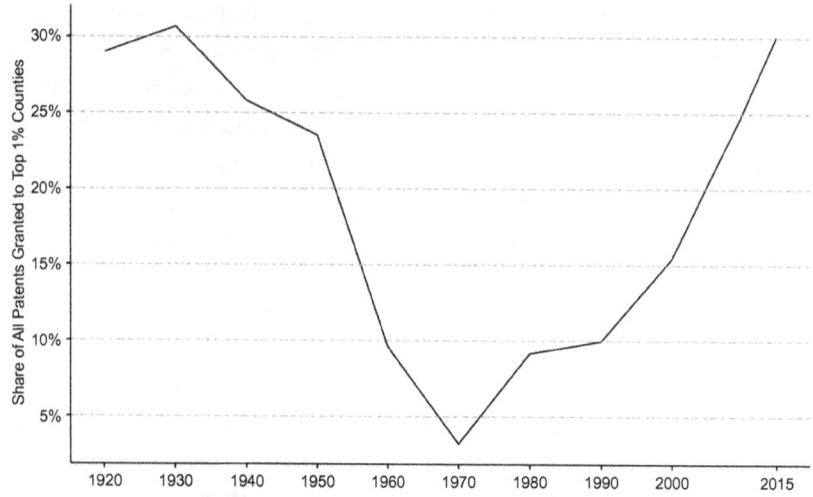

Figure 15 Percentage of all patents granted to the top 1% of counties by decade, 1920–2015

Notes: We calculate patents per capita at the county level relying on patent grant data from Histpat and the USPTO and then divide them by county-level population estimates from the US Census for the years graphed: 1920, 1930, 1940, 1950, 1960, 1970, 1990, 2000, 2010, and 2015 (population data is only available in decadal increments from the US Census before 1970). We determine the top 1% of innovative counties by calculating the 99% percentile of counties in patents per capita granted in the decades graphed. We then calculate the share of all patents each year granted to the top 1% of innovative counties as determined by patents per capita. We note that in 1907 Oklahoma joined the union; in 1912, New Mexico and Arizona joined; and in 1959, both Hawaii and Alaska joined. Omitting Hawaii and Alaska does not materially alter the patterns depicted in the graph.

Sources: Histpat (Petralia, Ballard, and Rigby 2016); USPTO, US Census; authors' calculations.

9.2 American Populism

American populism is not a fixed ideology but, rather, a nimble and protean political style or strategy (Judis 2016; Kazin 1998; Mudde 2004). Populists seek to attain popular support by pitting the common people, often depicted as a virtuous, silent majority, against corrupt, if not degenerate, elites (Mudde 2004). Hence, populists do not share a message or policy program per se, but rather represent or mobilize groups that perceive themselves to be ignored by mainstream political forces.

While some populists may promote class warfare and redistribution, others may pit the interests of native-born citizens – the "pure people" – against those of immigrants and seek to exclude the latter from the benefits of citizenship, including social insurance and welfare transfers. Others may take the side of "ordinary citizens" in their efforts to resist exploitative policies enacted by elites (Judis 2016; Kazin 1998).

In the United States, populism is a perennial political force that has resurfaced historically and is often anti-intellectual and anti-statist (Judis 2016; Kazin 1998). American populists typically buck the established consensus on the economic issues of their day and advance economic policy in line with the preferences of their "marginalized" constituencies, often directly antagonizing and vilifying those economic sectors associated with the "elite." They have historically politicized new issues and forced mainstream parties to change their own positions by co-opting them (Kazin 1998). Many have espoused nativist, nationalist, protectionist, and isolationist policy agendas. In doing so, they have often championed policies that threatened the innovation clusters of their time and, conversely, appealed to innovation deserts.

While there have been many political movements and parties in the United States that have been branded as populists by pundits and academics, including the Know-Nothings, the Greenback Party, and the Populist Party, the most notable and impactful populist before the 1990s was William Jennings Bryan.[123] Once a leading figure in the Democratic Party, he ran unsuccessfully as that party's presidential nominee in 1896, 1900, and 1908.

Bryan championed farmers' economic interests. He capitalized politically on the fact that during the late 1870s and early 1900s, they had suffered significantly from price deflation for their agricultural commodities; faced increased transportation prices; and experienced unemployment and reduced wages due to an influx of immigrants, farming sector consolidation, and mechanization. Small farmers, in particular, were weighed down by high debt loads and experienced mass foreclosures (Judis 2016; Kazin 1998).

Bryan lionized a romanticized agrarian golden age and was extremely critical of the economic, social, and political changes wrought by increased industrialization (Kazin 1998). He railed against "corrupt" big cities, especially older, established ones on the eastern seaboard, industrialists, railroad barons, and big banks (Judis 2016). During his presidential campaigns, Bryan called for looser monetary policy (so-called bimetallism or the free coinage of silver) to help

---

[123] The list of American populists includes colorful figures such as Huey Long, who was the governor of Louisiana between 1928 and 1932 and taxed the rich to fund education, infrastructure projects, and improvements to healthcare; Father Coughlin, who attacked Wall Street and was virulently anti-Semitic while pitting the interests of common people against bankers and financiers, and George Wallace, a racist governor of Alabama who ran for president four times during the 1960s and 1970s, three times as a Democrat, and once as a candidate for the American Independent Party, and who railed against "pointy-headed intellectuals" and "briefcase-toting bureaucrats" during these campaigns.

reduce farmers' real debt burdens; favored stronger antitrust laws and regulations targeted at railroads; and sought to constrain banks from financing land speculation while championing depositor insurance (Kazin 1998).[124]

In advancing this agenda, Bryan appealed to places that were rural and less innovative compared to more urban areas economically oriented toward the leading economic sectors of their time. Contra Trump, however, for Bryan championing "the people" meant opposing tariffs on competing imports, which during the early 1900s benefited places that were relatively industrialized because, despite raising consumer prices, they sheltered American-made products such as textiles, machines, and firearms. Moreover, Bryan differed from Trump in the fact that he did not explicitly speak out against the innovation clusters of his day or put forth policy proposals that necessarily pitted these places against places that were less innovative. Next, we adduce evidence for a more nebulous relationship between geographic innovation inequality and populism during the Bryan era.

Figure 16 shows the geographical variation in the electoral appeal of Bryan in the 1908 presidential election across the continental United States. We graph the share of the Democratic two-party vote. There are some notable similarities between the geographic voting patterns represented by this figure and those associated with the 2016 presidential election (see Figure 6). As with the 2016 race and the counties that supported Trump, rural areas, and those that were not necessarily the innovation clusters of their day, including big cities in the Southern states such as New Orleans, seem to be overrepresented vis-à-vis their support for Bryan. This is especially true for those counties located within the extremely fertile, cotton-producing areas of the Southern "Black Belt," which is not entirely surprising since the Democratic Party explicitly courted segregationists during this period.

While Figure 16 suggests a negative relationship between spatial innovation and support for Bryan's version of populism, it is certainly not dispositive. Therefore, similar to Sections 7 and 8, where we evaluated the relationship between innovation at the county level and Trumpism (in 2016 and 2020, respectively), Table 7 displays the results of several regressions that examine the association between innovation, measured as Patents Per Capita in 1900, and support for Bryan's presidential campaigns in 1900 and 1908, respectively, measured as a share of the two major parties that contested those two elections (the Republicans and Democrats).[125] As in Sections 7 and 8, we proceed from the simplest specification to the most complex.

---

[124] Bryan also supported progressive policies such as a progressive income tax, stronger labor rights, and several like-minded political reforms.

[125] We use historical patent grant data from Histpat and aggregate these by the county of the first-named inventor. We note that we are missing information on a relatively large number of

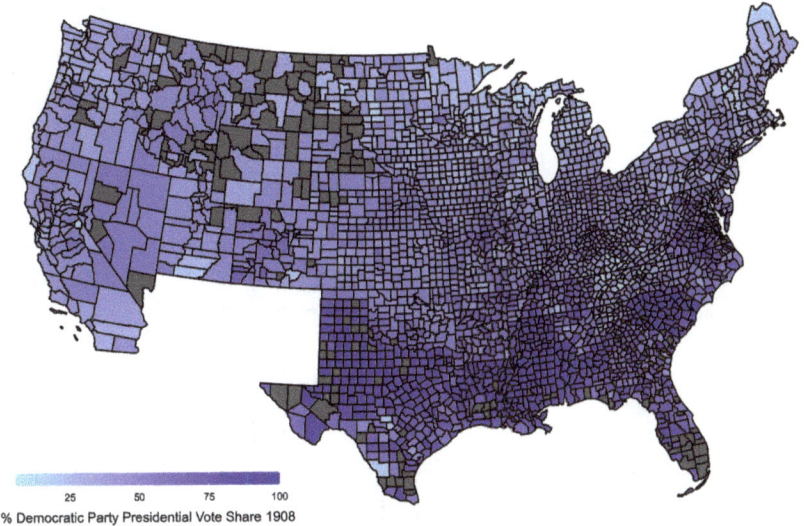

Figure 16 William Jennings Bryan county-level vote share in 1908 in the continental United States

Note: We calculate the vote share of Bryan in 1908 as the two-party vote share at the county level achieved by the Democratic Party. New Mexico and Arizona did not join the Union until 1912. The Democratic two-party vote share has 115 missing values in 1908; these are depicted as dark gray.
Source: Amlani and Alrgara (2021).

In Column 1, we report the results of a simple bivariate linear model estimated via OLS. As was the case in Sections 7 and 8, higher levels of innovation are associated with less electoral success for populism, in this case measured as Bryan's early twentieth-century version: increasing log(Patents Per Capita) by 1% decreases Bryan's share of the 1900 two-party presidential vote by 1.9 percentage points (p-value = 0.001). The r-squared is only .03, however.

In Column 2, we report the second-stage results of a regression estimated via IV on the same dependent variable, Bryan's vote share in 1900. The only independent variable in that regression is the estimate (predicted values) of log (Per Capita Patents) generated by the first stage regression represented by equation 1 in Section 7. While we omit the results of the first stage regression here, we note that, identical to Table 1, Column 2a, we estimated a model that predicts values of log(Patents Per Capita) as a function of the instruments we

---

counties compared to the main analyses presented in Sections 7 and 8. If we consider the missing values for the dependent variable as well, then 1,587 counties are included in the 1900 regressions and 1,614 counties in the 1908 regressions (out of a total of 2,980 existing counties that year). However, we note that the results in Table 7 do not change materially if we instead recode the missing patent data as zeroes.

Table 7 The determinants of Bryan's populism

	(1)	(2)	(3)	(4)	(5)	(6)
Election Year	1900	1900	1900	1908	1908	1908
Regression Approach	OLS	IV	IV	OLS	IV	IV
log(Patents Per Capita)	−1.906***	−5.567**	1.233	−2.838***	−7.007***	0.015
	[0.749]	[2.606]	[1.855]	[0.820]	[1.848]	[1.538]
State-Fixed Effects	No	No	Yes	No	No	Yes
Observations	1,587	1,587	1,587	1,614	1,614	1,614

Notes: Significant at the 0.01 level (***); significant at the 0.05 level (**); significant at the 0.10 level (*). Patents per capita is measured in 1900. We calculate "Populism" by calculating the two-party Democratic vote share in 1900 and 1908. We estimate, but do not report, several first-stage regression results for the regressions estimated via IV. We cluster the standard errors across all models by commuting zone and weigh the observations by counties' total votes in the 1900 and 1908 presidential elections, respectively.

introduced in Section 6 and deployed in Sections 7 and 8: Temperature, Precipitation, and Population Density, all measured in 1900. As was the case when we moved from an estimation strategy based on OLS to one based on IV in Sections 7 and 8, the Column 2 results are much stronger than those obtained in Column 1: increasing patents per capita by 1% decreases Bryan's share of the 1900 two-party presidential vote by 5.6 percentage points (p-value = 0.001).

In Column 3, we add state-fixed effects to the regression represented by Column 2. This circumscribes the county-level variation to only that within states, rather than between states; while the coefficient for Patents Per Capita is now positive, it is statistically insignificant (p-value = 0.51). Therefore, we can surmise that, at best, the relationship between spatial innovation and populism as represented by Bryan's 1900 electoral campaign is mixed.

Columns 4 to 6 repeat the same structure represented by Columns 1 to 3, except that the dependent variable is now Bryan's share of the presidential vote in 1908. The results of these regressions mirror those obtained for the 1900 election. While Columns 4 and 5 show strong evidence for the claim that more innovation means less support for populism, Column 6 implies that this finding does not hold within states, only across them.

9.3 Increasing Salience of the Innovation Cleavage Feeds Perot's Populism

As early as 1944, Senator Harley Kilgore, a Democrat from West Virginia, voiced concerns about the uneven distribution of federal R&D spending that was emerging during World War II, a pattern we documented and discussed earlier in this section (see Figure 15). He sought to narrow the geographic inequality in technological creation and commercialization, a gulf partially engendered by policies that favored certain regions, universities, and firms (Gross and Sampat 2020; Kevles 1977; Short 2022). As we discussed in Section 6, a host of federal policies did indeed help to attenuate American innovation inequality, at least temporarily (see Figures 8 and 15).

Ultimately, though, a more "elitist" postwar research funding model advanced by Vannevar Bush prevailed. It ignored most of Kilgore's suggestions (Short 2022) and was partially responsible for the resurgence of innovation inequality after 1970 exhibited in Figure 15. This thus reinforced patterns that were potentially ripe for populist exploitation and set the stage for Trump's enhanced ability to use innovation inequality as a politically powerful wedge issue.

During the Cold War, the federal government and armed forces funneled billions of dollars in grants into basic research around lasers, the Global Positioning

System (GPS), and semiconductors, especially in efforts to outfit missiles with precision-guided weapons and land humans on the moon. This meant awarding NSF grants to scientists working in major research universities and generously financing the Defense Advanced Research Projects Agency (DARPA), which was housed in the Pentagon and funded basic research at universities and corporate research parks and helped create an interconnected research network (Mazzucato 2011). Prominent examples of publicly subsidized organizations include the Stanford Research Institute, the Lincoln Laboratory, a military-funded research center affiliated with MIT, and the Rand Corporation in Santa Monica, California (O'Mara 2005; Wright 2020).

While R&D spending associated with OSRD during World War II and subsequent Cold War R&D spending helped to boost the innovative prospects of a few locations that had previously been innovation deserts, it also turbocharged areas that were already relatively innovative (see Gross and Sampat 2020; Wright 2020). Over 87% of all 1960 military contracts went to firms in just 185 different counties (Isard 1962). This included places such as Boston, Massachusetts, home to MIT, and New Jersey, home to several Bell Labs facilities, where transistors and other computer-age technologies were first developed.

Consider the West Coast. Data on Prime Military Contracts from 1960 shows that 12.5% of all federal defense spending flowed to Los Angeles County in California alone (Isard 1962). Southern California was already the leader in US aircraft manufacturing, so this only compounded its economic edge as a huge influx of skilled workers, defense contracts, and federal R&D spending spilled over to other firms in the region (Gross and Sampat 2020; Wright 2020). The greater Seattle region also benefited from this pattern, thanks in part to Boeing's outsized role in producing seaplanes during World War I and military aircraft during World War II, as did Northern California's south bay around Stanford University and San Diego (O'Mara 2005; Wright 2020).

Meanwhile, several already established cities on the Eastern seaboard also benefited from increased support from the federal government during this period as it showered several leading universities and research labs with public money in its efforts to crack encrypted messages, develop radar, and pioneer the Atomic Bomb, among other technologies with national defense implications (O'Mara 2020, 2005). Take just one example: the University of Pennsylvania was home to the first electronic, general-purpose digital computer, the Electronic Numerical Integrator and Computer (ENIAC), which came online in 1945 and was heavily subsidized by the US Army to help calculate ballistic missile trajectories. Its creators then founded a company in Philadelphia that developed the first general-purpose computer, the Universal Automatic Computer (UNIVAC), for the commercial market.

This sequence of events presaged a pattern that would repeat itself throughout the Third Industrial Revolution: early during the Cold War, the federal government deployed grants and subsidies, and undertook technology transfer efforts and procurement policies that primed certain places to successfully commercialize new goods and services during the 1970s and 1980s (Mazzucato 2011; O'Mara 2020; Weiss 2014). Entrepreneurs and firms located near national laboratories and leading universities that received considerable federal funding were able to bring hardware and software breakthroughs to market and convert them into lucrative profits with a considerable lag, long after the federal government's first efforts to stimulate R&D around semiconductors, telecommunications, and satellites, or to serve as a buyer of first resort for those products (Mazzucato 2011; Weiss 2014).

The commercialization of computer-age goods and services was not relegated only to entrenched companies. To be sure, large, established, and vertically integrated firms such as AT&T, Xerox, IBM, and Hewlett Packard helped introduce several new technologies, including the personal computer and its trappings, such as the mouse. However, the rise of venture capital and growing importance of the stock market for helping public companies raise capital meant that several new firms such as Apple Computers capitalized on the growing appetite by households and businesses for digital technologies. With a few notable exceptions such as Compaq Computer, which was founded in Houston, TX, before it was purchased by Hewlett Packard in 2002, these firms were born in extant innovation clusters (see O'Mara 2020).

By 1990, the commercialization of computers and the infrastructure that would eventually culminate in the World Wide Web was in full swing. The numbers around R&D spending bespeak the transition from the initial, basic science stages of the Third Industrial Revolution, embodied by the introduction of the integrated circuit in 1959, to the introduction of the mass-produced personal computer in the late 1970s. Recall that Figure 7 (in Section 6) documents both private R&D (%GDP) conducted by US businesses and public R&D (%GDP) conducted by the federal government between 1953 and 2021. It shows that, while R&D as a share of the economy almost doubled between 1953 and 1965, circa 1980 private R&D funding surpassed public funding. As a result, we would expect the cleavage between less innovative and more innovative areas to have become more politically important by the early 1990s.

Enter Ross Perot, a political outsider who championed an eclectic mix of policies that cut across conventional ideological differences. His agenda included reducing the federal deficit and shrinking the national debt through a balanced budget amendment to the Constitution, tax reform, and spending cuts; curbing the influence of lobbyists and special interest groups; imposing term limits on federal legislators; and experimenting with new forms of direct democracy such as electronic town halls (Judis 2016). In doing so, Perot turned to the populist playbook by engaging in antiestablishment rhetoric and appealing to the common man and woman through a folksy and down-to-earth manner.

Like Bryan before him, Perot further complicates the pre-Trump era relationship between populism and innovation, however. Before he ran for president as an independent in both 1992 and 1996, Perot was the founder of Electronic Data Systems (EDS) and Perot Systems, both of which were at the forefront of data processing and information technology services during the 1980s. During his presidential runs, Perot advocated for improving US education around science, technology, engineering, and mathematics (STEM); was a proponent of investing in R&D and high-tech sectors; and championed entrepreneurship and risk-taking.

However, Perot, like Trump, opposed economic globalization championed by both major political parties at the time. He was extremely skeptical of free trade in general and NAFTA in particular (Judis 2016). Perot argued that by encouraging companies to employ cheaper labor in the Global South, freer trade would accelerate the outsourcing of blue-collar manufacturing jobs.

Like Trump after him, this stance potentially threatened more innovative places that, by the late 1980s and early 1990s, were populated with firms that had already begun to specialize in software and other activities centered on intangible capital (O'Mara 2020). By this time, the vertical disintegration of several goods, characterized by varying degrees of separation between R&D, design, testing, assembly, packaging, marketing, and retail, began to take hold and birthed global supply chains. This phenomenon included products such as personal computers and electronic equipment manufactured in Japan and South Korea that ran on American software powered by both American and foreign microchips (see Miller 2022; O'Mara 2020). It also included automobiles; companies such as Ford opened plants in Mexico and Canada during this time and exported vehicles to the United States, with plans to open more factories in these US neighbors if NAFTA were to be ratified.

To evaluate the relationship between spatial innovation and support for Perot, and similar to Sections 7 and 8, where we evaluated the relationship between innovation and Trumpism at the county level (in 2016 and 2020, respectively),

Table 8 Historical innovation and electoral support for Perot

PANEL A	(1)	(2)	(3)	(4)	(5)
Patents Data Year	1976	1977	1978	1979	1980
log(Patents Per Capita)	−4.209	−4.163	−4.891	−3.478*	−3.944*
	[2.813]	[2.556]	[3.416]	[1.911]	[2.320]
Observations	2,812	2,812	2,812	2,812	2,812
PANEL B	(6)	(7)	(8)	(9)	(10)
Patents Data Year	1981	1982	1983	1984	1985
log(Patents Per Capita)	−4.154*	−3.680*	−3.922*	−4.583	−3.702*
	[2.480]	[2.031]	[2.419]	[3.113]	[2.084]
Observations	2,812	2,812	2,812	2,812	2,812
PANEL C	(11)	(12)	(13)	(14)	(15)
Patents Data Year	1986	1987	1988	1989	1990
log(Patents Per Capita)	−4.067*	−4.005*	−3.913*	−4.266*	−4.143*
	[2.395]	[2.317]	[2.289]	[2.471]	[2.451]
Observations	2,660	2,660	2,660	2,653	2,653

Notes: Significant at the 0.01 level (***); significant at the 0.05 level (**); significant at the 0.10 level (*). Patents Per Capita is measured in 1976, 1977, 1978, 1979, 1980, 1981, 1982, 1983, 1984, 1985, 1986, 1987, 1988, 1989, and 1990. We calculate "Electoral Support for Perot" by calculating the vote share achieved by Ross Perot for all votes cast in the 1992 presidential elections. We estimate, but do not report, several first-stage regression results for the IV models. We cluster the standard errors across all models by commuting zone and weigh the observations by counties' total votes in the 1992 presidential elections.

as well as between innovation and support for Bryan's presidential campaigns in 1900 and 1908 (Table 7), we explore whether a similar relationship exists for Perot's presidential campaigns.[126] Table 8 reports the results of a series of regressions estimated via IV where we look at the county-level relationship between logged(Patents Per Capita) and support for Perot in 1992 as a share of all presidential votes cast.[127] Across each column, we report the second-stage results on Perot's vote share for regressions that also include state-fixed effects.[128] The independent variable of interest in each regression is the estimate

---

[126] We use USPTO data to operationalize patents per capita for each year between 1976 and 1990. We note that we are missing information on some counties but that the results do not change materially if we instead recode the missing patent data as zeroes.

[127] The data on Perot's county level electoral returns are from David Leip's Election Atlas.

[128] While we reran all the regressions for Perot's electoral support in the 1996 presidential election as well and note that they are materially similar to those contained in Table 8, we do not report them here.

(predicted values) of log(Per Capita Patents) generated by the first stage regression represented by equation 1 in Section 7.[129]

Given the increasing salience over time of innovation inequality outlined earlier, we expect that places with fewer patents per capita closer in time to the 1992 election should be more likely to support Perot. Therefore, we report fifteen separate regressions where patents per capita are estimated for each yearly interval between 1976 and 1990: 1976 (Column 1), 1977 (Column 2), 1978 (Column 3), 1979 (Column 4), 1980 (Column 5), 1981 (Column 6), 1982 (Column 7), 1983 (Column 8), 1984 (Column 9), 1985 (Column 10), 1986 (Column 11), 1987 (Column 12), 1988 (Column 13), 1989 (Column 14), and 1990 (Column 15).

The crux of Table 8's regression results: Perot's brand of populism is less likely to map onto the geography of innovation than Trump's did in both 2016 and 2020, ratifying the idea that, unlike Perot, by the 2010s Trump was able to politically benefit from higher levels of innovation inequality that were more politically salient. While in general more innovative counties, captured by their patents per capita, were less likely to vote for Perot, this relationship never achieves a level of statistical significance better than 10% and the substantive magnitude of the effect for the regressions that are statistically significant at this level is much lower than what we uncover for Trump in 2016. Namely, consider a cognate model estimated via IV with state-fixed effects and no baseline controls reported in Table 1, Column 6: while the coefficient on Patents Per Capita from that Trump regression is -6.097 (p-value < 0.001), the average of the Patents Per Capita coefficients for the statistically significant (at the 10% level) Perot regressions is -3.934.[130]

As expected, we find that the estimated negative effect of innovation on support for Perot gets *stronger* as we measure innovation closer in time. We note that while across all the regressions reported in Table 8 the sign on the Patents Per Capita coefficient is always negative, suggesting less support for Perot in more innovative counties, this effect only becomes statistically significant at the 10% level when we measure patents in 1979 or later. And if we compare the coefficient for Patent Per Capita that year (Column 4) to the coefficient for Patent Per Capita measured in 1989 (Column 14), the effect is 19% stronger in the later period.

---

[129] While we omit the results of the first stage regression in Table 8, we note that, identical to Table 1, Column 2a, we estimated a model that predicts values of log(Patents Per Capita) as a function of the instruments we introduced in Section 6 and deployed in Sections 7 and 8 and Table 7 in this section: Temperature, Precipitation and Population Density, all measured in 1900.

[130] The statistically significant coefficients are the ones depicted in Column 4, Column 5, Column 6, Column 7, Column 8, Column 10, Column 11, Column 12, Column 13, and Column 14.

We submit that innovation inequality may be mapping onto greater support for populism closer to Perot's first presidential run because it is becoming more politically salient throughout the 1980s and early 1990s. The logical conclusion is that by the time Trump runs for president in 2016, innovation inequality is much higher and much more politically salient; thus, electoral support for Trump in low-innovation places is significantly greater than it was for Perot. Next, we elaborate on why both innovation inequality and its salience increased further after the early 1990s.

9.4 Why Did Trump Exploit Innovation Inequality Better Than Previous Populists?

As Figure 15 clearly shows, while US innovation inequality increased in 1970, it ballooned since around 2000. Only a handful of places emerged as clear winners in the digital economy as measured by their contributions to innovation. Figure 17 graphs the number of counties where 500 or more patents were granted (per year) between 1920 and 2015. It shows that innovation clusters have grown more innovative over time, widening the gap between themselves

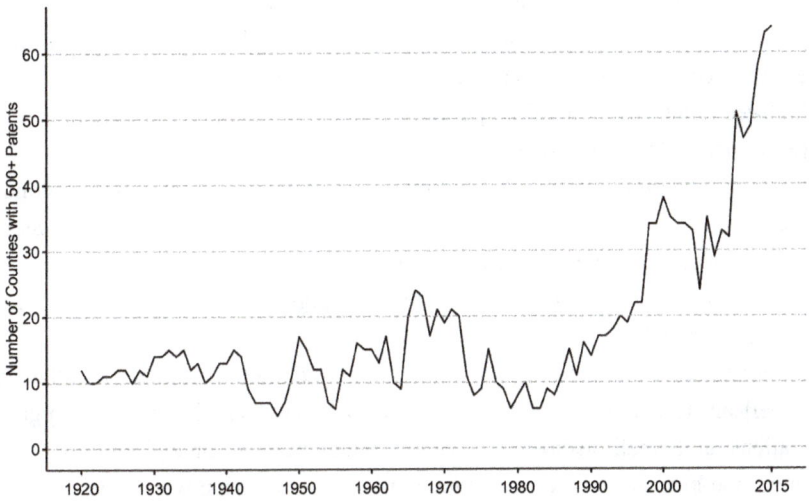

Figure 17 Total number of counties granted 500+ patents per year, 1920–2015

Note: We calculate the number of counties that were granted 500 or more patents in any given year between 1920 and 2015 by relying on patent grant data from Histpat and the USPTO. We note that in 1907 Oklahoma joined the union; in 1912, New Mexico and Arizona joined; and in 1959, both Hawaii and Alaska joined. Omitting Hawaii and Alaska does not materially alter the patterns depicted in the graph.

Sources: Histpat (Petralia, Ballard, and Rigby 2016); USPTO; authors' calculations.

and less innovative places. While the number of "superstar counties" with 500 or more patents doubled between World War II and 1970, only to recede during the 1980s, they exploded in frequency after the Cold War. And since the early 2000s, the number of superstar counties has dramatically increased. While there were only 6 counties that received 500 or more patents in 1979, there were over 60 of them in 2015.

Other facts bear this pattern out. Between 1920 and 2015, the median number of patents awarded to each county barely budged, while the average increased dramatically after 1980. This suggests that counties at the high end of the distribution are patenting substantially more. This is corroborated by the fact that the top 1% of innovative counties monopolize a greater share of the granted patents since 1990 as time transpires (this pattern is depicted in Figure 15). Consider that 1,083 counties out of 3,143 (34.5%) in 2015 were not granted any patents at all and 1,995 counties in 2015 were granted fewer than 5 patents. Moreover, 2,800 counties out of 3,143 (89.1%) were granted fewer than the average number of patents that year, which was 49.

The rest of this section is dedicated to shining light on why American innovation inequality has exploded during the twenty-first century, as well as exploring reasons for its heightened political salience and susceptibility to populist exploitation. Primarily, several late twentieth-century policies favored stronger IP rights and increased the value of intangible capital. In turn, this engendered a stronger bifurcation between design and manufacturing for both high-tech devices and other goods centered on globalized supply chains (Schwartz 2021; Short 2022).

What were these policies? First, they include domestic reforms to IP. Second, the liberalization of trade and the inclusion of stronger IP protection in international trade agreements. Third, more market-friendly antitrust policies incentivized the commercialization of the internet, digital platforms, and AI (Pistor 2019; Short 2022).

During the late 1970s and early 1980s, several domestic reforms strengthened American IP. The Bayh-Dole Act of 1980 allowed universities, nonprofit organizations, and small businesses to secure patent rights to inventions developed under the auspices of federally funded research programs, which incentivized more patenting, licensing, and the commercialization of inventions (Stevens 2004). The Economic Recovery Tax Act of 1981 reduced taxes on income generated from the sale or licensing of patents and decreased taxes on capital gains, which benefited venture capital investors and those who purchased shares in publicly traded technology firms. The introduction of the US Court of Appeals for the Federal Circuit in 1982, which seats judges who specialize in IP matters, provided more standardized, reliable expert decisions about patent suit appeals.

These reforms effectively circumvented courts that had hitherto provided rulings more skeptical of patents (Pistor 2019; Short 2022).

In turn, this bequeathed inventors and investors with stronger IP rights that were more certain, whose validity was upheld more often, and who were awarded injunctive relief with greater frequency when courts ruled their patents were infringed upon, therefore encouraging greater commercialization of innovation (see Short 2022). Furthermore, the USPTO improved its patent examination process to accommodate more technically sophisticated patents around semiconductors and software, setting the stage for an increase in the overall volume of patent applications (Galetovic 2021).

After the Cold War, the United States also consolidated an international system that promoted international trade, capital flows, and technology transfer. In part, it was intended to allow developed countries to better allocate capital and focus on their comparative advantage around intangible and human capital, including design, software, IP, R&D, and marketing. During the 1990s, tariffs were cut in half and stronger IP was written into multilateral and bilateral trade agreements.

In 1994, President Clinton signed the Uruguay Round Agreement Acts, which converted GATT into the WTO and bound member nations to the Agreement on Trade-Related Aspect of IPRs known as TRIPS (see Drahos and Braithwaite 2002). TRIPS substantially strengthened global patent protection for US IP producers abroad by spreading standardized, stronger IP rules to the developing world (Sell 2003). The United States also strengthened global IP protection through bilateral and multilateral trade deals such as NAFTA and the TPP.

The apotheosis of twenty-first-century globalization was when China joined the WTO in 2001. To be sure, the Doha Round of global tariff negotiations collapsed during the mid-2000s because several countries did not want to reduce barriers to agricultural imports. However, a strong bipartisan consensus prevailed in the United States around the idea that China and the US should increase their economic interdependence, in part to help American firms gain access to the expanding Chinese market (see Hung 2021).

While federal R&D as a percentage of GDP has declined substantially since 1980 (see Figure 7), innovative areas have continued to benefit from a variety of policies intended to boost US performance in advanced technologies (see Block 2018; Mazzucato 2011, Weiss 2014). As we already outlined, IP legislation from the 1980s allows universities and private companies to retain exclusive property rights to inventions that emerge from R&D that is wholly or partly funded by the federal government (Bayh-Dole and Stevenson-Wydler Acts). This has substantially reduced their R&D costs and allowed them to exploit increasingly valuable patent portfolios. Moreover, many elite research universities located in already prosperous innovation clusters have been partly transformed into business incubators that transfer technology to fledgling start-ups and even incumbent firms. The universities themselves benefit from tax breaks and often receive large grants from the NSF, NIH, or other federal agencies (Mettler 2011).

Separately, the ability of the US to secure international cooperation over enhanced IP enforcement in venues such as the WTO has been particularly important for globalizing US innovation. It has allowed American firms to generate profits from their intangible capital, including branding, R&D, and the commercialization of novel technologies (Schwartz 2019, 2021). The biggest beneficiaries include Apple, Microsoft, Oracle, Intel, IBM, Cisco Systems, Pfizer, Johnson & Johnson, and Procter & Gamble (Forbes 2022). Figure 18, which graphs American IP exports between 1970 and 2015, points to the increasing economic predominance of intangible capital, especially since the start of the twenty-first century. Indeed, during this period the United States became the largest exporter of ideas and high value-added services (Menaldo and Wittstock 2021).

Moreover, the profits of many if not most innovative US firms today rest on complicated, vertically disintegrated global supply chains (Schwartz 2019, 2021). This calls on them to import and export all manner of

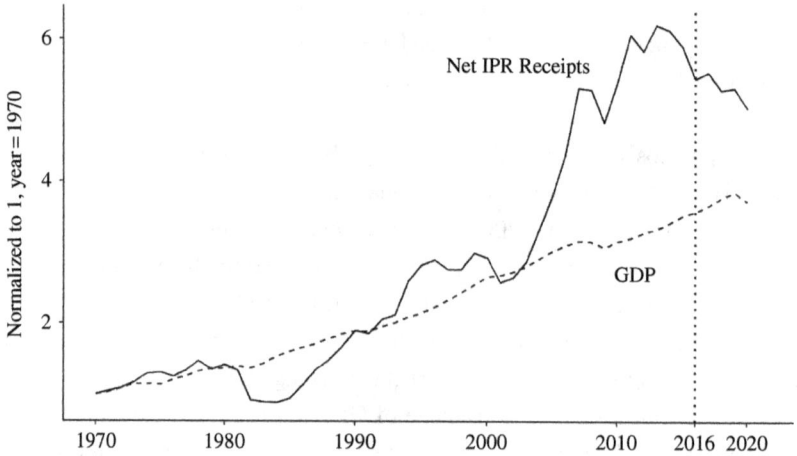

Figure 18 US net receipts of IP payments compared to US GDP, 1970–2015

Notes: Net IP receipts are obtained by subtracting incoming receipts from outgoing payments measured in 2010 dollars. GDP is expressed in 2010 dollars. Both are normalized to 1970, which equals 1. The vertical line, 2016, marks the election of Donald Trump to the US presidency.

Source: *IMF Balance of Payments Statistics Yearbook* and data files.

raw materials, intermediate inputs, and finished goods and services. It also means they need to rely on relatively free international capital flows and the international enforcement of their IP as imports and inbound FDI may help introduce them to new technologies from abroad in the form of machinery, intermediary goods, and finished products. This is even the case when the exporting country is relatively technologically unsophisticated (Menaldo 2021; Menaldo and Wittstock 2021). And indeed, rules-based globalization based on reduced tariffs, capital liberalization, and the international protection of IP helped foster the creation and commercialization of electronic devices produced in global supply chains, nurturing an app-based economy centered on digital platforms, big data, and AI (Menaldo and Wittstock 2021).

In addition, important reforms to antitrust and communications policy also helped catalyze this new technological and economic paradigm. Economists, legal scholars, and judges challenged three pillars of the progressive, Brandeisian antitrust tradition that had dominated competition policy over the majority of the twentieth century. First, the per se reading of antitrust laws that had issued blanket prohibitions against certain economic models and strategies. Second, the tendency to shield specific competitors from bigger or newer rivals instead of fostering competition. Third, structural theories about the linear relationship between industry concentration and market power, which assumed that fewer, bigger firms automatically mean higher prices and the potential to monopolize markets.

During the 1970s and 1980s, more market-oriented intellectual and ideological movements influenced courts, which were gradually adopting a more textualist interpretation of both the Sherman and Clayton Acts while embracing cost-benefit analysis rooted in the quantifiable evidence of consumer harm (see Chen, Ash, and Naidu 2022). Taken together, these changes ushered in a "consumer welfare" approach to competition policy that tolerated, if not encouraged, larger scale and new business models associated with the digital revolution. In turn, high-tech firms were allowed to reach demand-side economies of scale, engage in countless mergers and acquisitions, and experiment with different degrees of vertical integration.

In this vein, as we outlined in Section 4, the supply chain for semiconductors became extremely specialized and globalized. It was transformed into a completely vertically disintegrated process where design, fabrication, testing, assembly, and packaging are separated. Moreover, the software and machinery needed for each step in the production process is made by specialized companies, many of them located outside the United States (Miller 2022). The leading chip design firms are American, while the hegemonic manufacturer is TSMC, a Taiwanese firm. The leading lithographic equipment maker is

ASML, a Dutch firm. South Korean firms, meanwhile, specialize in making memory chips.

Being able to coordinate complex supply chains that span countries is essential for these highly innovative firms since semiconductors are subject to technological changes tied to accelerated product cycles that proceed at breakneck speed. This is especially true when it comes to AI chips. In turn, this appreciably compounds the risks of an industrial organization strategy vested in vertical integration within the four corners of the United States that implies high fixed capital investments.

Additionally, the introduction of the iPhone consolidated seemingly impregnable network effects in multi-sided markets across search, social networks, internet commerce, and gig economy industries such as ridesharing and vacation rentals. This has reinforced the technological edge of innovation clusters that attract high levels of venture capital and witnessed the birth of new firms competing in these novel industries. These clusters are located in states such as California, North Carolina, and New England.

As we also explained in Section 4, workers who have benefited from this development include both skilled and unskilled laborers who live and work in innovation clusters. This is especially true for places that host firms that export their high value-added goods and services abroad. Yet, people living outside of these areas do not necessarily benefit directly from the success that highly innovative US companies enjoy globally. As we explained in Section 4 and earlier, many of these companies have outsourced manufacturing abroad, which means that areas outside of innovation clusters do not receive spillover growth.

The political consequences of these policy changes and their geographic impact took some time to materialize, however. Because the direction and pace of innovation were appreciably different before the internet, digital platforms, and AI, there was less room for a populist politician to exploit more muted and less salient geographic innovation inequality. Earlier Big Tech firms such as AT&T, Xerox, and IBM were vertically integrated and their manufacturing footprint was overwhelmingly located in the United States. Even though there was innovation inequality during the Cold War, places that were more technologically isolated were still economically integrated into the supply chains for high-tech products such as semiconductors and computers and defense-related products such as missiles and aircraft and satellites. As a result, innovation hubs within the United States were engines of manufacturing networks with a heavy footprint stateside. This meant that innovation inequality was not as economically impactful or politically salient because the economic interests of people outside of innovation clusters were more aligned with those within them.

Trump therefore accelerated, but did not necessarily cause, the evolution of the Republican Party from pro-business and largely pro-innovation to one that is, for lack of a better term, populist in a Trumpian fashion (also see Ruffini 2023 on this point). President Reagan's economic platform was explicitly in favor of innovation and open to international trade, albeit with important exceptions, including tariffs on Japanese motorcycles. Now, most influential Republican lawmakers, and even including those in the upper house, are populist with a Trumpian accent. While they complain that digital platforms censor conservative voices and champion progressive cultural issues, Republican Senators Josh Hawley, Marco Rubio, J. D. Vance, and Steven Daines are some of the most notable politicians who favor "reining in" Big Tech, along with more militant House members such as James Comer and Jim Jordan.

These GOP lawmakers have increasingly advocated on behalf of blue-collar workers and unions and rail against free trade. Texas Governor Greg Abbott, along with the Republican-run state house, has barred the state from doing business with various asset managers and banks on the grounds that they shun fossil fuels and thus hurt workers employed in those industries. Changes in Republican campaign funding exemplify the populist ascendance, as most GOP donations are now in the form of small money contributions instead of corporate money from Political Action Committees.

10 Reflections on Populism and Polarization

In this Element, we show that relatively more innovative US counties were significantly less likely to support Trump during both the 2016 and 2020 presidential elections. We also explain the reasons why and explore how Trump was different in degree, but not kind, from earlier populists. In doing so, we make several theoretical and empirical contributions. We also raise several questions for future research.

10.1 Summarizing our Main Contributions

This Element documents how, during the 2016 presidential election, Candidate Trump touted the economic policy preferences of voters living in places outside of America's innovation clusters. He espoused trade protectionism, restrictions on capital and technological flows, and an industrial strategy tailored to subsidize American suppliers in specific industries. Trump also spoke out directly against Big Tech companies. Unlike Hillary Clinton in 2016 and Joe Biden in 2020, he neglected innovative firms' concerns around providing access to high-speed internet access, more immigration of highly skilled foreign workers, broadly investing in science and technology, and improving higher education. Trump's antipathy toward economic globalization and his promises to challenge the US-led, rules-based system of global trade and investment directly challenged the business models of America's most innovative firms.

We also show how Trump then pursued several policies that harmed innovation during his presidency. We submit that this alienated the high-tech community and may have induced voters in innovation clusters in battleground states such as Arizona and Georgia to flip their support toward the Democrats and, in turn, helped elevate Biden to the presidency in 2020. We find strong evidence that the 2016 pattern of innovation clusters rejecting Trumpism was repeated during the 2020 presidential election.

We introduce a theoretical framework that brings together several strands of ideas to help explain why Trumpist policies pose such a threat to American innovators and those places deriving direct economic benefits from their activities. This includes making sense of things such as the aggregate economic benefits of trade and who supports globalization in developed countries and why. We explain why American firms operating in high-tech sectors such as software, hardware, machinery, vehicles, biotechnology, aerospace, telecommunications, diagnostics, chemicals, and green energy benefit from trade, international capital flows, vibrant technology transfer across borders, and stronger IP globally. We extended the logic to their workers and communities.

We also explain why those living and working outside of innovation clusters do not necessarily directly benefit from policies preferred by innovative places and may therefore be open to populist attacks on "globalism." Innovative US companies have been able to specialize along a comparative advantage rooted in innovating at breakneck speeds, but more so around design than manufacturing, and exploiting intangible capital, all while choreographing international supply chains. As a result, the domestic industrial footprint generated by innovative US firms has been substantially reduced. The corresponding divergence in economic interests between innovation hubs and deserts, paired with the dramatic increases in innovation inequality since 1970 that we document, makes it unsurprising that politicians such as Trump would capitalize on this socioeconomic cleavage.

We corroborate this theoretical framework empirically. The Element's main finding, that innovative places strongly rejected Trumpism, in both the 2016 and 2020 presidential elections, is resilient to alternative specifications. This includes measuring Trumpism and innovation in different ways and introducing different sets of potentially confounding variables, including controlling for Chinese import exposure shocks – and specifications where we instrument these. It is also robust to introducing state-fixed effects, indirectly and directly testing for whether the exclusion restriction is satisfied, for example, by controlling for exposure to robots directly and through an instrument, dropping major innovation clusters, conducting adjustments for spatial correlation, and most importantly, instrumenting innovation, which we measure using patents per capita. We introduce and defend a suite of exogenous demographic, geographical, and climatic features that the literature documents as important for the origin of technology clusters in the United States. We find as well that places with increased patenting activity between presidential elections saw reductions in Trump's campaign contributions and electoral support.

Following Haber, Elis, and Horrillo (2022), we provide evidence that relatively temperate climates partly determined the location of innovation clusters in the United States. We show that these differences have endured, and that the technological gulf between less innovative and more innovative places has grown over time. We also outline the reasons for the self-reinforcing nature of American innovation clusters.

We also trace and discuss changes in innovation inequality over the long run. We outline how innovation inequality follows a U-shaped pattern over the long twentieth century. While it was relatively high at the turn of the twentieth century, federal government programs during World War II and especially the Cold War helped to appreciably reduce it via aggressive government funding and coordinating of basic science and R&D due to national security exigencies and Cold War politics. However, these efforts ran out of steam by 1970 when innovation inequality increased again and, by the turn of the twenty-first century, was supercharged by a digital economy rooted in vertically disintegrated global supply chains and network effects that reinforced existing geographic disparities. By the time Trump won the 2016 election, the US landscape was dotted with a few innovation oases surrounded by manifold innovation deserts.

To the best of our knowledge, our Element is the first to show that the economic reasons why voters supported Trump across two presidential elections go beyond the loss of jobs and income due to trade with China and increased automation and associated downward mobility. Rather, it is because of something broader and not necessarily spatially correlated with these factors: a major rift in economic policy preferences and thus support for Trump and populism in the United States today exists between more and less innovative areas. Regardless of their demographics, exposure to trade and robots, education and income levels, degree of urbanization, and every other potential difference between them, innovation clusters oppose Trump, and his policies, and innovation deserts support him, and his populist agenda.

We also investigate whether the historical evolution of innovation inequality we document is connected to the recurring historical phenomenon of American populism. We find a weak, albeit consistent association between innovation inequality and geographic variation in support for populism at the presidential level prior to 2016. We argue that innovation inequality is a more politically salient and divisive issue today: not only was there relatively less innovation inequality in the recent past, but even when it was quite high, it occurred in a radically different American political economy. It took several policies, such as reforms to domestic and international IP, to help usher in the rise of the current leading US economic sectors centered on generating and commercializing knowledge and technology (pharmaceuticals, biotechnology, semiconductors, software, personal electronics, and computers) for innovation differences to really pack a political punch, readymade for a political entrepreneur such as Trump to exploit.

10.2 Directions for Future Research

While this Element adduces strong path dependence in America's innovation-intensive regions over time, economic policy preferences did not necessarily stratify so strongly along geographic lines in past periods. And past populists were not as successful as Trump in turning geographic differences, be they economic or cultural, into political fuel. Nowadays, American voters increasingly appear to have more divergent political preferences than ever before, with many of them expressed along geographic lines. Perhaps growing cultural and political polarization may incline voters in less innovative places toward more reactionary politics in general: not only trade protectionism and opposition to immigration, but antipathy toward "liberal cultural issues" that may include science and technology (Abramowitz 2010; Baldasarri and Gelman 2008; Bishop 2009).

Future research may examine this question, as well as other issues raised by our findings. Does the negative relationship between innovation and populism hold for legislative elections and/or state and local level elections? Does it hold in different countries and for different time periods?

We show that innovation inequality between regions in the United States has dramatically increased since 1970, yet this dynamic may reverse in the future. Indeed, in the wake of the remote work revolution induced by the Covid-19 pandemic, key differences between US locations may attenuate into the future (Muro and You 2022). Office occupancy rates in downtown business districts across the United States continue to be depressed, remaining at historically low levels (Weber, Grant, and Hoffman 2022). As concerns over crime, safety, and quality of life issues such as growing commute times have exploded in cities such as New York City, Chicago, Washington, D.C., San Francisco, Los Angeles, and Seattle, alongside skyrocketing housing costs, many of their highly skilled residents have fled to Florida, Texas, and the

American interior. Most have not sought out innovation clusters, but instead moved to suburbs and even rural areas with slower paces of life, predominantly in so-called red states (see Mitchell 2022). Moreover, as we intimate in Section 1, President Biden's aggressive industrial policies may bear some fruit in reducing innovation inequality, similar to federal investment during the Cold War, which we document in Section 6.

We cannot really predict what political impacts this phenomenon may have. Perhaps a slackening in the rate of innovation inequality between American locations may reduce polarization, or at least herald the return of convergence over economic policy? Perhaps this may mirror the Cold War consensus about the government's role in promoting innovation to include both public spending and the support of markets, including globalization (O'Mara 2020)?

Of course, given that it is highly unlikely that the sharp differences between US voters regarding economic policy, and especially around innovation, are entirely due to spatial divergences in technological development alone, this consensus is unlikely to reemerge any time soon. Trumpism may therefore continue to hold sway, with or without the former president's return to the Oval Office in 2024.

References

Abramovitz, Moses. 1993. "The Search for the Sources of Growth: Areas of Ignorance, Old and New." *The Journal of Economic History* 53(2): 217–243.

Abramowitz, Alan. 2010. *The Disappearing Center: Engaged Citizens, Polarization, and American Democracy*. New Haven: Yale University Press.

Acemoglu, Daron, and Pascual Restrepo. 2020. "Robots and Jobs: Evidence from US Labor Markets." *Journal of Political Economy* 128(6): 2188–2244.

Acemoglu, Daron, Jacob Moscona, and James Robinson. 2016. "State Capacity and American Technology: Evidence from the Nineteenth Century." *American Economic Review* 106(5): 61–67.

Acemoglu, Daron, David Autor, David Dorn, Gordon Hanson, and Brendan Price. 2016. "Import Competition and the Great Us Employment Sag of the 2000s." *Journal of Labor Economics* 34(1): 141–198.

Acs, Zoltan, Luc Anselin, and Attila Luc. 2002. "Patents and Innovation Counts as Measures of Regional Production of New Knowledge." *Research Policy* 31(7): 1069–1085.

Amlani, Sharif, and Carlos Algara. 2021. "Partisanship & Nationalization in American Elections: Evidence from Presidential, Senatorial, & Gubernatorial Elections in The US Counties, 1872–2020." *Electoral Studies* 73: 102387.

Anelli, Massimo, Italo Colantone, and Piero Stanig. 2019. "We Were the Robots: Automation and Voting Behavior in Western Europe." *BAFFI CAREFIN Centre Research Paper* 2019-115.

Atkinson Robert, Doug Brake, Daniel Castro, et al. 2020. "Trump vs. Biden: Comparing the Candidates' Positions on Technology and Innovation." *Information Technology and Innovation Foundation*: Washington, DC.

Atkinson, Robert, Mark Muro, and Jacob Whiton. 2019. "The Case for Growth Centers." *Brookings Institution*: Washington, DC.

Autor, David, David Dorn, and Gordon Hanson. 2013a. "The China Syndrome: Local Labor Market Effects of Import Competition in The United States." *American Economic Review* 103(6): 2121–2168.

Autor, David, David Dorn, and Gordon Hanson. 2013b. "The Geography of Trade and Technology Shocks in The United States." *American Economic Review* 103(3): 220–225.

Autor, David, David Dorn, and Gordon Hanson. 2015. "Untangling Trade and Technology: Evidence from Local Labor Markets." *The Economic Journal* 125(584): 621–646.

Autor, David, David Dorn, and Gordon Hanson. 2016. "The China Shock: Learning from Labor-Market Adjustment to Large Changes in Trade." *Annual Review of Economics* 8: 205–240.

Autor, David, David Dorn, Gordon Hanson, and Jae Song. 2014. "Trade Adjustment: Worker-Level Evidence." *The Quarterly Journal of Economics* 129(4): 1799–1860.

Autor, David, David Dorn, and Gordon Hanson. 2019. "When work disappears: Manufacturing decline and the falling marriage market value of young men." *American Economic Review: Insights* 1(2): 161–178.

Autor, David, David Dorn, Gordon Hanson, and Kaveh Majlesi. 2020. "Importing Political Polarization? The Electoral Consequences of Rising Trade Exposure." *American Economic Review* 110(10): 3139–3183.

Baccini, Leonardo, and Stephen Weymouth. 2021. "Gone for Good: Deindustrialization, White Voter Backlash, and US Presidential Voting." *American Political Science Review* 115(2): 550–567.

Baccini, Leonardo, Mattia Guidi, Arlo Poletti, and Aydin Yildirim. 2022. "Trade Liberalization and Labor Market Institutions." *International Organization* 76(1): 70–104.

Bade, Avin. 2021. "White House Debates to Delay Biden's Plan for Tariffs on Key Chinese Industries." *Politico*. www.politico.com/news/2021/10/29/white-house-tariffs-china-517727.

Bakker, Gerben, Nicholas Crafts, and Pieter Woltjer. 2017. "The Sources of Growth in a Technologically Progressive Economy." *GGDC Research Memorandum No. GD-156*. Groningen Growth and Development Centre, University of Groningen.

Baldassarri, Delia, and Andrew Gelman. 2008. "Partisans without Constraint: Political Polarization and Trends in American Public Opinion." *American Journal of Sociology* 114(2): 408–446.

Ball State University. 2022. "Study Identifies Most Likely Locations for Semiconductor Plants in US." techxplore.com.

Barret, Malachi. 2020. "Biden Says Trump Failed to Bring Back Michigan Jobs and Tanked Economy with COVID Response." *MLive*. www.mlive.com/public-interest/2020/09/biden-says-trump-failed-to-bring-back-michigan-jobs-and-tanked-economy-with-covid-response.html.

Batistich, Mary Kate, and Timothy Bond. 2019. "Stalled Racial Progress and Japanese Trade in the 1970s and 1980s." *IZA Discussion Manuscript No. 12133*.

BBC. 2016. "Trump Accuses China of 'Raping' U.S. with Unfair Trade Policy." *BBC News*. www.bbc.com/news/election-us-2016-36185012.

Bergh, Andreas, and Therese Nilsson. 2010. "Do Liberalization and Globalization Increase Income Inequality?" *European Journal of Political Economy* 26(4): 488–505.

Bessen, James. 2015. *Learning by Doing*. New Haven: Yale University Press.

Biden, Joe. 2020. "The Biden Plan to Rebuild US Supply Chains and Ensure the US Does Not Face Future Shortages of Critical Equipment." https://joebiden.com/supplychains/.

Bishop, Bill. 2009. *The Big Sort: Why the Clustering of Like-Minded America is Tearing us Apart*. Boston: Houghton Mifflin Harcourt.

Blau, Francine, and Christopher Mackie. 2016. "National Academies of Sciences, Engineering, and Medicine." *The Economic and Fiscal Consequences of Immigration: A Report*. Washington, DC

Blinken, Antony. 2021. "A Foreign Policy for the American People." www.state.gov/a-foreign-policy-for-the-american-people/.

Block, Fred. 2018. "Swimming against the Current: The Rise of a Hidden Developmental State in the United States." *Politics & Society* 36(2): 169–206.

Boix, Carles. 2019. *Democratic Capitalism at the Crossroads: Technological Change and the Future of Politics*. Princeton: Princeton University Press.

Bonacich, Edna, and Khaleelah Hardie. 2006. "Walmart and the Logistics Revolution." In *Wal-Mart: The Face of Twenty-First-Century Capitalism*, ed., Nelson Lichtenstein. New York: The New Press: 163–187.

Breschi, Stefano, and Francesco Lissoni. 2003. "Mobility and Social Networks: Localized Knowledge Spillovers Revisited." *Università commerciale Luigi Bocconi*.

Broz, Lawrence, Jeffry Frieden, and Stephen Weymouth. 2021. "Populism in Place: The Economic Geography of the Globalization Backlash." *International Organization* 75(2): 464–494.

Buggle, Johannes, and Ruben Durante. 2021. "Climate Risk, Cooperation and the Co-Evolution of Culture and Institutions." *The Economic Journal* 131(637): 1947–1987.

Bureau of Economic Analysis. www.bea.gov/.

Bush, Vannevar. 1945. *Science, the Endless Frontier*. Princeton: Princeton University Press.

Carey, Kevin. 2016. "Donald Trump Doesn't Understand Common Core (and Neither Do His Rivals)." *The New York Times*. www.nytimes.com/2016/03/08/upshot/donald-trump-doesnt-understand-common-core-and-neither-do-his-rivals.html.

Casper, Steven, 2007. "How Do Technology Clusters Emerge and Become Sustainable?: Social Network Formation and Inter-Firm Mobility within The San Diego Biotechnology Cluster." *Research Policy* 36(4): 438–455.

Çelik, Sadullah, and Ulkem Basdas. 2010. "How Does Globalization Affect Income Inequality? A Panel Data Analysis." *International Advances in Economic Research* 16(4): 358–370.

Che, Lu, Justin Pierce, Peter Schott, and Zhigang Tao. 2016. "Does Trade Liberalization with China Influence US Elections?" No. w22178. *National Bureau of Economic Research*.

Chen, Daniel, Elliott Ash, and Suresh Naidu. 2022. *Ideas Have Consequences: The Impact of Law and Economics on American Justice*. No. 22–1392. Toulouse School of Economics.

Choi, Jiwon, Ilyana Kuziemko, Ebonya Washington, and Gavin Wright. 2021. "Local Economic and Political Effects of Trade Deals: Evidence from NAFTA." No. w29525. *National Bureau of Economic Research*.

Clark, Paul. 2017. "Presidential Election: The Pivotal Role of Pennsylvania and the Rustbelt." *Labor Studies Journal* 42(3): 239–244.

Clayton, James, 1967. "The Impact of the Cold War on the Economies of California and Utah, 1946–1965." *Pacific Historical Review* 36(4): 449–473.

Clinton, Hillary. 2015. "Being Pro-Business Doesn't Mean Hanging Consumers out To Dry." *Quartz*. https://qz.com/529303/hillary-clinton-being-pro-business-doesnt-mean-hanging-consumers-out-to-dry.

Co, Catherine, 2002. "Evolution of the Geography of Innovation: Evidence from Patent Data." *Growth and Change* 33(4): 393–423.

Cohn, Nate. 2016a. "Why Trump Won: Working-Class Whites." *New York Times*. www.nytimes.com/2016/11/10/upshot/why-trump-won-working-class-whites.html.

Cohn, Nate. 2016b. "How Trump's Campaign Could Redraw Voter Allegiances." *New York Times*. www.nytimes.com/2016/06/30/upshot/how-trumps-campaign-could-redraw-voter-allegiances.html.

Colantone, Italo, and Piero Stanig. 2018a. "Global Competition and Brexit." *American Political Science Review* 112(2): 201–218.

Colantone, Italo, and Piero Stanig. 2018b. "The Trade Origins of Economic Nationalism: Import Competition and Voting Behavior in Western Europe." *American Journal of Political Science* 62(4): 936–953.

Conley, Brian. 2018. "Thinking What He Says: Market Research and the Making of Donald Trump's 2016 Presidential Campaign." In *Political Marketing in the 2016 US Presidential Election*, ed., Jamie Gillies. New York: Palgrave Macmillan: 29–48.

Conley, Timothy G. (1999). "GMM Estimation with Cross Sectional Dependence." *Journal of Econometrics* 92(1): 1–45.

Conley, Timothy, Christian Hansen, and Peter Rossi. 2012. "Plausibly Exogenous." *The Review of Economics and Statistics* 94(1): 260–272.

Corradini, Carlo, 2021. "The Geography of Innovation as Reflected by Social Media." *Environment and Planning A: Economy and Space* 53(2): 227–229.

Cramer, Kathy. 2016. *The Politics of Resentment: Rural Consciousness in Wisconsin and the rise of Scott Walker.* Chicago: University of Chicago Press.

Crump, Jeff, and Clark Archer. 1993. "Spatial and Temporal Variability in the Geography of American Defense Outlays." *Political Geography* 12(1): 38–63.

David, Paul A. 1990. "The dynamo and the computer: an historical perspective on the modern productivity paradox." *The American Economic Review* 80(2): 355–361.

David, Paul and Gavin Wright. 1997. "Increasing Returns and the Genesis of American Resource Abundance." *Industrial and Corporate Change* 6(2): 203–245.

Davidson, Adam. 2016. "Blaming Trade and Voting Trump in the Rust Belt." *New York Times Magazine*. www.nytimes.com/2016/07/10/magazine/blaming-trade-and-voting-trump-in-the-rust-belt.html.

De Bromhead, Alan, Barry Eichengreen, and Kevin H. O'Rourke. 2013. "Political Extremism in the 1920s and 1930s: Do German Lessons Generalize?" *The Journal of Economic History* 73(2): 371–406.

Deng, Ping, Andrew Delios, and Mike W. Peng. 2020. "A geographic relational perspective on the internationalization of emerging market firms." *Journal of International Business Studies* 51: 50–71.

Di Tella, Rafael, and Dani Rodrik . 2020. "Labor Market Shocks and the Demand for Trade Protection: Evidence from Online Surveys." *The Economic Journal* 130(628): 1008–1030.

Diamond, Jeremy. 2016. "Trump: 'We Can't Continue to Allow China to Rape Our Country.'" *CNN Politics*. www.cnn.com/2016/05/01/politics/donald-trump-china-rape/index.html.

Dinlersoz, Emin, and Zoltan Wolf. 2018. "Automation, Labor Share, and Productivity: Plant-Level Evidence from US Manufacturing." Unpublished Manuscript. https://ideas.repec.org/p/cen/wmanuscript/18-39.html.

Dippel, Christian, Robert Gold, Stephan Heblich, and Rodrigo Pinto. 2022. "The Effect of Trade on Workers and Voters." *The Economic Journal* 132(641): 199–217.

Dorn, David, Gordon Hanson, and Kaveh Majlesi. 2020. "Importing Political Polarization? The Electoral Consequences of Rising Trade Exposure." *American Economic Review* 110(10): 3139–3183.

Downes, Larry. 2016. "A Brief Review of Hillary Clinton's Innovation Plan." *Harvard Business Review*. https://hbr.org/2016/07/a-brief-review-of-hillary-clintons-innovation-plan.

Drahos, Peter, and John Braithwaite. 2002. *Information Feudalism: Who Owns the Knowledge Economy?* New York: Routledge Press.

The Economist. 2017. "Dealing with Donald: Donald Trump's Trade Bluster." *The Economist.* www.economist.com/briefing/2016/12/10/donald-trumps-trade-bluster.

The Economist. 2019. "America Still Leads in Technology, But China Is Catching up Fast." *The Economist.* www.economist.com/special-report/2019/05/16/america-still-leads-in-technology-but-china-is-catching-up-fast.

The Economist. 2021. "The New Order of Trade." *The Economist.* www.economist.com/special-report/2021/10/06/the-new-order-of-trade.

The Economist. 2023." New Industrial Policies Will Make the World More Unequal." www.economist.com/special-report/2023/10/02/new-industrial-policies-will-make-the-world-more-unequal.

Fabrizio, Lee, & Associates. 2020. "Post-Election Exit Poll Analysis – 10 Key Target States." www.politico.com/f/?id=00000177-6046-de2d-a57f-7a6e8c950000.

Federal Communications Commission. 2021. "FCC Revokes China Telecom America's Telecom Services Authority." *News Release.* www.fcc.gov/document/fcc-revokes-china-telecom-americas-telecom-services-authority.

Feler, Leo, and Mine Z. Senses. 2017. "Trade Shocks and the Provision of Local Public Goods." *American Economic Journal: Economic Policy* 9(4): 101–143.

Ferenstein, Gregory, 2016. "Tech Billionaires like Democrats More Than Republicans. Here's Why." *The Washington Post.* www.washingtonpost.com/posteverything/wp/2016/05/31/tech-billionaires-like-democrats-more-than-republicans-heres-why/.

Finch, Brian, Elizabeth Vella Moeller, Matthew Oresman, et al. 2020. Trump vs. Biden: Technology and the Internet. Pillsbury. www.pillsburylaw.com/en/news-and-insights/technology-policy-trump-biden-election.html.

Findlay, John. 1995. "Atomic Frontier Days Richland, Washington, and the Modern American West." *Journal of the West* 34(3): 32–41.

Forbes. 2022. The Global 2000. www.forbes.com/lists/global2000/?sh=8db90975ac04.

Freund, Caroline, and Dario Sidhu. 2017. "Global Competition and the Rise of China." *Peterson Institute for International Economics Working Manuscript* 17-3.

Frey, Carl Benedikt, Thor Berger, and Chinchih Chen. 2018. "Political Machinery: Did Robots Swing the 2016 US Presidential Election?." *Oxford Review of Economic Policy* 34(3): 418–442.

Fuller, Gregory, Alison Johnston, and Aidan Regan. 2020. "Housing Prices and Wealth Inequality in Western Europe." *West European Politics* 43(2): 297–320.

Galetovic, Alexander. 2021. "Patents in the History of the Semiconductor Industry." In *The Battle over Patents: History and Politics of Innovation*, eds., Stephen Haber and Naomi Lamoreaux. London: Oxford University Press: 27–68.

Galetovic, Alexander, and Stephen Haber. 2017. "The Fallacies of Patent-Holdup Theory." *Journal of Competition Law & Economics* 13(1): 1–44.

Gerber, Michelle. 1992. *On the Home Front: The Cold War Legacy of the Hanford Nuclear Site*. Lincoln: University of Nebraska Press.

Giuliano, Paola, and Nathan Nunn. 2021. "Understanding Cultural Persistence and Change." *The Review of Economic Studies* 88(4): 1541–1581.

Goldin, Claudia, and Lawrence Katz. 2009. *The Race between Education and Technology*. Cambridge, MA: Harvard University Press.

Goos, Maarten, Alan Manning, and Anna Salomons. 2014. "Explaining Job Polarization: Routine-Biased Technological Change and Offshoring." *American Economic Review* 104(8): 2509–2526.

Gordon, Robert. 2017. *The Rise and Fall of American Growth: The US Standard of Living since the Civil War*. Princeton: Princeton University Press.

Grammich, Clifford, Kirk Hadaway, Richard Houseal, et al. 2012. "2010 US Religion Census: Religious Congregations & Membership Study." *Association of Statisticians of American Religious Bodies*. www.usreligioncensus.org/images/2010_US_Religion_Census_Introduction.pdf.

Grassegger, Hannes, and Mikael Krogerus. 2017. "The Data That Turned the World upside down." *Motherboard*. https://motherboard.vice.com/en_us/article/how-our-likes-helped-trump-win.

Green, Jon, and Sean McElwee. 2019. "The Differential Effects of Economic Conditions and Racial Attitudes in the Election of Donald Trump." *Perspectives on Politics* 17(2): 358–379.

Green, Joshua, and Sasha Issenberg. 2016. "Inside the Trump Bunker, with Days to Go." *Bloomberg*. www.bloomberg.com/news/articles/2016-10-27/inside-the-trump-bunker-with-12-days-to-go.

Greene, Daniel. 2021. *The Promise of Access: Technology, Inequality, and the Political Economy of Hope*. Cambridge, MA: MIT Press.

Greenstein, Shane. 2010. "Innovative Conduct in Computing and Internet Markets." In *Handbook of the Economics of Innovation*, eds., Bronwyn H. Hall and Nathan Rosenberg. Vol. 1. Amsterdam: North-Holland: 477–537.

Griffin, Robert, and Ruy Teixeira. 2017. "The Story of Trump's Appeal: A Portrait of Trump Voters." *The Democracy Fund Voter Group*. www.voterstudygroup.org/publication/story-of-trumps-appeal.

Grim, Ryan, Nick Baumann, and Matt Fuller. 2016. "At Secretive Meeting, Tech CEOs and Top Republicans Commiserate," Plot to Stop Trump.

www.huffpost.com/entry/aei-world-forum-donald-trump_n_56ddbd38e4b0ffe6f8ea125d.

Gros, Daniel. 2013. "Why Does Capital Flow from Poor to Rich Countries?" *Vox EU*. https://voxeu.org/article/why-does-capital-flow-poor-rich-countries.

Gross, Daniel, and Bhaven Sampat. 2020. "Inventing the Endless Frontier: The Effects of the World War II Research Effort on Post-war Innovation." (No. w27375). *National Bureau of Economic Research*.

Gross, Daniel, and Bhaven Sampat. 2023. "America, Jump-Started: World War II R&D and the Takeoff of the US Innovation System." *American Economic Review* 113(12): 3323–3356.

Gruber, Jonathan, and Simon Johnson. 2019. *Jump-Starting America: How Breakthrough Science Can Revive Economic Growth and the American Dream*. London: Hachette UK.

Guriev, Sergei, and Ellias Papaioannou. 2022. "The Political Economy of Populism." *Journal of Economic Literature* 60(3): 753–832.

Haber, Stephen, Roy Elis, and Jordan Horrillo. 2022. "The Ecological Origins of Economic and Political Systems." http://dx.doi.org/10.2139/ssrn.3958073.

Hahn, Jinyong, and Jerry Hausman. 2003. "Weak Instruments: Diagnosis and Cures in Empirical Econometrics." *American Economic Review* 93(2): 118–125.

Hakobyan, Shushanik, and John McLaren. 2016. "Looking for Local Labor Market Effects of NAFTA." *Review of Economics and Statistics* 98(4): 728–741.

Hean, Oudom, and Mark Partridge. 2021. "The Impact of Metropolitan Technology on the Non-Metropolitan Labor Market: Evidence from US Patents." *Regional Studies* 56(3): 476–488.

Hejny, Jessica. 2018. "The Trump Administration and Environmental Policy: Reagan Redux?." *Journal of Environmental Studies and Sciences* 8(2): 197–211.

Hill, Seth, Daniel Hopkins, and Gregory Huber. 2019. "Local Demographic Changes and US Presidential Voting, 2012 to 2016." *Proceedings of the National Academy of Sciences* 116(50): 25023–25028.

Hiscox, Michael. 2002. "Commerce, Coalitions, and Factor Mobility: Evidence from Congressional Votes on Trade Legislation." *American Political Science Review* 96(3): 593–608.

Hope, Bradley. 2016. "Inside Donald Trump's Data Analytics Team on Election Night." *Wall Street Journal*. www.wsj.com/articles/inside-donald-trumps-data-analytics-team-on-election-night-1478725225.

Howe, Peter D., Matto Mildenberger, Jennifer R. Marlon, and Anthony Leiserowitz. 2015. "Geographic Variation in Opinions on Climate Change at State and Local Scales in the USA." *Nature Climate Change* 5(6): 596–603.

Hull, Katy. 2020. "Lost and Found: Trump, Biden, and White Working-Class Voters." *Atlantisch Perspectief* 44(5): 11–16.

Hung, Ho-Fung. 2022. *Clash of Empires: From Chimerica to the New Cold War*. Cambridge: Cambridge University Press.

Hurt, Shelley. 2015. "The Military's Hidden Hand: Examining the Dual-use Origins of Biotechnology in the American Context, 1969–1972." In *State of Innovation: The Politics of Knowledge Production in the Modern Era*, eds., Fred L. Block and Matthew R. Keller. New York: Routledge: 31–56.

Im, Zhen Jie, Nonna Mayer, Bruno Palier, and Jan Rovny. 2019. "The Losers of Automation': A Reservoir of Votes for the Radical Right?" *Research & Politics* 6(1): 2053168018822395.

Irwin, Douglas. 2017. *Clashing over Commerce*. Chicago: University of Chicago Press.

Isard, Walter. 1962. *Awards of Prime Military Contracts by County, State and Metropolitan Area of the United States, Fiscal Year 1960*. Regional Science Research Institute.

Iversen, Torben, and David Soskice. 2020. *Democracy and Prosperity: Reinventing Capitalism through a Turbulent Century*. Princeton: Princeton University Press.

Jacoby, Wade. 2020. "Surplus Germany." *German Politics* 29(3): 498–521.

Judis, John. 2016. *The Populist Explosion: How the Great Recession Transformed American and European Politics*. New York: Columbia Global Reports.

Judis, John and Ruy Teixeira. 2023. *Where Have All the Democrats Gone? The Soul of the Party in the Age of Extremes*. New York: Henry Holt.

Karl, Thomas, and Walter Koss. 1984. "Regional and National Monthly, Seasonal and Annual Temperature Weighted by Area, 1895–1983." *Historical Climatology Series 4–3*.

Kazin, Michael. 1998. *The Populist Persuasion: An American History*. Cornell: Cornell University Press.

Kerr, William, and Ramana Nanda. 2013. "Location Choice for New Ventures: Cities." *Harvard Business School Entrepreneurial Management Case*. Cambridge, MA: Harvard University Press.

Kevles, Daniel. 1977. "Foundation and the Debate over Postwar Research Policy." *Isis* 68(241): 5–26.

Khalifa, Sherif. 2022. *Geography and the Wealth of Nations*. Lanham: Rowman & Littlefield.

Kim, In Song. 2017. "Political Cleavages within Industry: Firm-level Lobbying for Trade Liberalization." *American Political Science Review* 111(1): 1–20.

Kosseff, Jeff. 2019. *The Twenty-Six Words that Created the Internet*. Cornell: Cornell University Press.

Lamoreaux, Naomi, and Kenneth Sokoloff. 2007. "Introduction: The Organization and Finance of Innovation in American History." In *Financing Innovation in the United States, 1870 to Present*, eds., Naomi Lamoreaux and Kenneth Sokoloff. Cambridge, MA: The MIT Press: 1–38.

Lapowsky, Issie. 2016. "Trump's Plan for American-Made iPhones Would Be Disastrous." *Wired Magazine*. www.wired.com/2016/03/trump-wont-get-apple-make-iphones-shouldnt/.

Lapowsky, Issie. 2018. "The Lasting Impacts of Trump's First Year." *Wired*. www.wired.com/story/trump-first-year-impact-on-innovation/.

Leduc, Sylvain, and Zheng Liu. 2023. "Automation, Bargaining Power, and Labor Market Fluctuations." *American Economic Journal: Macroeconomics*.

Lee, Michelle. 2016. "Donald Trump Flip-Flops, then Flips and Flops More on H-1B Visas." *The Washington Post*. www.washingtonpost.com/news/fact-checker/wp/2016/03/21/donald-trump-flip-flops-then-flips-and-flops-more-on-h-1b-visas/.

Leibovici, Fernando, and Jason Dunn. 2022. "U.S. Trade of Semiconductors: Cross-Country Patterns and Historical Dynamics." *Economic Synopses* (31): 1–3.

Leip, David. 1992. *Dave Leip's Atlas of U.S. Presidential Elections*. http://uselectionatlas.org.

Leip, David. 1996. *Dave Leip's Atlas of U.S. Presidential Elections*. http://uselectionatlas.org.

Mariotti, Sergio. 2022. "A Warning from the Russian–Ukrainian War: Avoiding a Future that Rhymes with the Past." *Journal of Industrial and Business Economics* 49(4): 761–782.

Markusen, Ann, and Robert Bloch. 1985. "Defensive Cities: Military Spending, High Technology and Human Settlements." *High Technology, Space and Society*: 106–120.

Marshall, Alfred, and Mary Paley Marshall. 1920. *The Economics of Industry*. London: Macmillan.

Mazzucato, Maria, 2011. *The Entrepreneurial State*. London: Penguin Random House.

McQuarrie, Michael. 2017. "The Revolt of the Rust Belt: Place and Politics in the Age of Anger." *The British Journal of Sociology* 68(1): 120–152.

Menaldo, Victor. 2021. "Do Patents Foster International Technology Transfer?" In *The Battle Over Patents: History and Politics of Innovation*, eds., Stephen Haber and Naomi Lamoreaux. London: Oxford University Press: 69–111.

Menaldo, Victor, and Nicolas Wittstock. 2021. "Does Technology Transfer from the US to China Harm American Firms, Workers, and Consumers? A Historical and Analytic Investigation." *Economic and Political Studies* 9(4): 417–446.

Mervis, Jeffrey. 2018. "Trump Emphasizes Workforce Training in New Vision for STEM Education." *Science*. www.science.org/content/article/trump-emphasizes-workforce-training-new-vision-stem-education.

Mettler, Suzanne. 2011. *The Submerged State: How Invisible Government Policies Undermine American Democracy.* Chicago: University of Chicago Press.

Miller, Chris. 2022. *Chip War: The Fight for the World's Most Critical Technology.* New York: Simon and Schuster.

Mitchell, Josh. 2022. "Red States Are Winning the Post-Pandemic Economy. *Wall Street Journal.* www.wsj.com/articles/red-states-winning-post-pandemic-economy-migration-11657030536.

Moretti, Enrico. 2012. *The New Geography of Jobs.* Boston: Houghton Mifflin Harcourt.

Morgan, Stephen, and Jiwon Lee. 2018. "Trump Voters and the White Working Class." *Sociological Science* 5: 234–245.

Mudde, Cas. 2004. The Populist Zeitgeist. *Government and Opposition 39*(4): 541–563.

Mullins, Brody. 2023. "How Republicans and Big Business Broke up." *The Wall Street Journal.* www.wsj.com/articles/republicans-corporations-donations-pacs-9b5b202b.

Muro, Mark, and Yang You. 2022. "Superstars, Rising Stars, and the Rest: Pandemic Trends and Shifts in The Geography of Tech." *Brookings Institution.* www.brookings.edu/research/superstars-rising-stars-and-the-rest-pandemic-trends-and-shifts-in-the-geography-of-tech/.

Muro, Mark, Robert Maxim, and Jacob Whiton. 2019. "Automation and Artificial Intelligence: How Machines are Affecting People and Places." *Brookings Institution.* https://onwork.edu.au/bibitem/2019-Muro,M-Maxim,R-etal-Automation+and+artificial+intelligence+How+machines+are+affecting+people+and+places/.

Mutz, Diana. 2018. "Status Threat, Not Economic Hardship, Explains the 2016 Presidential Vote." *Proceedings of the National Academy of Sciences* 115(19): E4330–E4339.

National Academy of Sciences. 1995. *Committee on Criteria for Federal Support of Research and Development.* Washington, DC: National Academies Press.

National Science Foundation. *History.* https://new.nsf.gov/about/history.

Nellis, Stephen, Alexandra Alper, Diane Bartz, and Karen Freifeld. 2019. "US Chipmakers Quietly Lobby to Ease Huawei Ban." *Reuters*. www.reuters.com/article/us-huawei-tech-usa-lobbying/us-chipmakers-quietly-lobby-to-ease-huawei-ban-sources-idUSKCN1TH0VA.

Nelson, Richard, and Gavin Wright. 1992. "The Rise and Fall of American Technological Leadership: The Postwar Era in Historical Perspective." *Journal of Economic Literature* 30(4): 1931–1964.

Nevo, Aviv, and Adam Rosen. 2012. "Identification with Imperfect Instruments." *Review of Economics and Statistics* 94(3): 659–671.

O'Mara, Margaret. 2005. *Cities of Knowledge: Cold War Science and the Search for the Next Silicon Valley: Cold War Science and the Search for the Next Silicon Valley.* Princeton: Princeton University Press.

O'Mara, Margaret, 2020. *The Code: Silicon Valley and the Remaking of America.* New York: Penguin Press.

O'Mara, M. (2022). The Gilded Elevator: TECH IN THE TIME OF TRUMP. In *The Presidency of Donald J. Trump: A First Historical Assessment*, ed. J. E. Zelizer. Princeton University Press: 219–237. https://doi.org/10.2307/j.ctv201xj05.15.

O'Rourke, Kevin. 2001. "Globalization and Inequality: Historical Trends. 2002." *Annual World Bank Conference on Development Economics.* Washington, DC: 39–67.

Osgood, Iain. 2018. "Globalizing the Supply Chain: Firm and Industrial Support for US Trade Agreements." *International Organization* 72(2): 455–484.

Pacewicz, Josh. 2016. "Here's the Real Reason Rust Belt Cities and Towns Voted for Trump." *The Washington Post*. www.washingtonpost.com/news/monkey-cage/wp/2016/12/20/heres-the-real-reason-rust-belt-cities-and-towns-voted-for-trump/.

Palmer, Annie. 2020. "Jeff Bezos, Bill Gates, and Other Tech luminaries React to Biden's Victory." *CNBC*. www.cnbc.com/2020/11/07/jeff-bezos-bill-gates-and-other-tech-luminaries-react-to-biden-win.html.

Perlstein, Joanna. 2016. "Techies Donate to Clinton in Droves. To Trump? Not So Much." *Wired Magazine*. www.wired.com/2016/08/techies-donate-clinton-droves-trump-not-much/.

Petralia, Sergio, Pierre-Alexandre Balland, and David Rigby. 2016. "Unveiling the Geography of Historical Patents in the United States from 1836 to 1975." *Scientific Data* (3): 160074. https://doi.org/10.1038/sdata.2016.74.

Petrova, Maria, Gregor Schubert, and Pinar Yildirim. 2024. "Automation, Loss of Jobs, and Support for Populism." Mimeo, Wharton.

Piketty, Thomas. 2014. *Capital In the 21st Century.* Cambridge, MA: Harvard University Press.

Pistor, Katharina. 2019. *The Code of Capital: How the Law Creates Wealth and Inequality*. Princeton: Princeton University Press.

Porter, Michael. 1998. "Clusters and the New Economics of Competition." *Boston: Harvard Business Review* 76(6): 77–90.

Research Triangle Park. 2018. "The Transformative Impact of the Research Triangle Park – A Case Study." Research Triangle Park (rtp.org).

The Republican National Convention. 2016. *Republican Party Platform*. www.presidency.ucsb.edu/documents/2016-republican-party-platform.

Rho, Sungmin, and Michael Tomz. 2017. "Why Don't Trade Preferences Reflect Economic Self-Interest?" *International Organization* 71(1): 85–108.

Ritchie, Melinda, and Hye Young You. 2021. "Trump and Trade: Protectionist Politics and Redistributive Policy." *Journal of Politics* 83(2): 800–805.

Roberts, Billy. 2014. National Renewable Energy Laboratory. Solid Biomass in the United States. www.nrel.gov/gis/biomass.html. Accessed: March 25, 2022.

Rodden, Jonathan. 2019. *Why Cities Lose: The Deep Roots of the Urban-Rural Political Divide*. New York: Basic Books.

Rogowski, Ronald. 1987. "Political Cleavages and Changing Exposure to Trade." *American Political Science Review* 81(4): 1121–1137.

Romer, Paul, 1993. "Idea Gaps and Object Gaps in Economic Development." *Journal of Monetary Economics* 32(3): 543–573.

Romm, Tony. 2017. "How Donald Trump Crippled US Technology and Science Policy." *Vox*. www.vox.com/2017/3/31/15139966/trump-white-house-technology-science-policy.

Ruffini, Patrick. 2023. *Party of the People: Inside the Multiracial Populist Coalition Remaking the GOP*. New York: Simon & Schuster

Scheve, Kenneth, and Matthew Slaughter. 2001. "What Determines Individual Trade-Policy Preferences?" *Journal of International Economics* 54(2): 267–292.

Schrank, Andrew. 2015. "Green Capitalists in a Purple State: Sandia National Laboratories and the Renewable Energy Industry in New Mexico." In *State of Innovation: The Politics of Knowledge Production in the Modern Era*, eds., Fred L. Block and Matthew R. Keller. New York: Routledge: 96–108.

Schwartz, Herman Mark. 2019. "American Hegemony: Intellectual Property Rights, Dollar Centrality, and Infrastructural Power." *Review of International Political Economy* 26(3): 490–519.

Schwartz, Herman Mark. 2021. "Mo'patents, Mo'problems: Corporate Strategy, Structure, and Profitability in America's Political Economy." In *The American Political Economy: Politics, Markets, and Power*, eds., Jacob S. Hacker, Alexander Hertel-Fernandez, Paul Pierson, and Kathleen Thelen. Oxford: Oxford University Press: 247–269.

Sell, Susan. 2003. *Private Power, Public Law: The Globalization of Intellectual Property Rights*. Cambridge: Cambridge University Press.

Sherman, Gabriel. 2016. "Operation Trump: Inside the Most Unorthodox Campaign in Political History." *New York Magazine* 3. https://nymag.com/intelligencer/2016/04/inside-the-donald-trump-presidential-campaign.html.

Sherman, Ryne. 2018. "Personal Values and Support for Donald Trump during the 2016 US Presidential Primary." *Personality and Individual Differences* 128(1): 33–38.

Short, Nicholas. 2022. "The Politics of the American Knowledge Economy." *Studies in American Political Development* 36(1): 41–60.

Smith, David, and Eric Hanley. 2018. "The Anger Games: Who Voted for Donald Trump in the 2016 Election, and Why?" *Critical Sociology* 44(2): 195–212.

Stanton, Katie. 2016. "An Open Letter from Technology Sector Leaders on Donald Trump's Candidacy for President." *Medium*. https://medium.com/newco/an-open-letter-from-technology-sector-leaders-on-donald-trumps-candidacy-for-president-5bf734c159e4#.nfpczjhlq.

Stevens, Ashley. 2004. The Enactment of Bayh–Dole. *The Journal of Technology Transfer* 29(1): 93–99.

Stock, James, Jonathan Wright, and Motohiro Yogo. 2002. "A Survey of Weak Instruments and Weak Identification in Generalized Method of Moments." *Journal of Business & Economic Statistics* 20(4): 518–529.

Stolper, Wolfgang, and Paul Samuelson. 1941. "Protection and Real Wages." *The Review of Economic Studies* 9(1): 58–73.

Swanson, Ana. 2021. "In Washington, 'Free Trade' Is NO Longer Gospel." *The New York Times*. www.nytimes.com/2021/03/17/business/economy/free-trade-biden-tai.html.

Swisher, Kara, and Ina Fried. 2017. "Apple CEO Tim Cook on Trump's Muslim Ban: 'Apple Would Not Exist without Immigration . . . It is Not a Policy we Support.'" *Vox*. www.vox.com/2017/1/28/14425952/tim-cook-donald-trump.

Taylor, Edward, and Andreas Rinke. 2017. "Trump Threatens German Carmakers with 35 Percent US Import Tariff." *Reuters Business News*. www.reuters.com/article/us-usa-trump-germany-autos-idUKKBN1500VJ.

Tesler, Michael. 2016. *Post-Racial or Most-Racial? Race and Politics in the Obama Era*. Chicago: University of Chicago Press.

Thewissen, Stefan, and David Rueda. 2019. "Automation and the Welfare State: Technological Change as a Determinant of Redistribution Preferences." *Comparative Political Studies* 52(2): 171–208.

Trump, Donald. 2016a. "Donald Trump: Disappearing Middle Class Needs Better Deal on Trade." *USA Today*. www.usatoday.com/story/opinion/2016/

03/14/donald-trump-tpp-trade-american-manufacturing-jobs-workers-column/81728584/.

Trump, Donald. 2016b. Declaring American Economic Independence. Trump/Pence Campaign, June 28. www.donaldjtrump.com/press-releases/donald-j.-trump-addresses-re-declaring-our-american-independence.

Trump, Donald. 2016c. Campaign Speech in Arizona. Donald Trump's Full Immigration Speech, Annotated. *LA Times*. www.latimes.com/politics/la-na-pol-donald-trump-immigration-speech-transcript-20160831-snap-htmlstory.html.

The Trump Archive. www.thetrumparchive.com/. Accessed: March 5, 2022.

Tucker, Patrick, Michelle Torres, Betsy Sinclair, and Steven Smith. 2019. "Pathways to Trump: Republican Voters in 2016." *Electoral Studies* 61: 102035.

US Census Bureau (1931). 1930 Census: Volume 1. Population, Number and Distribution of Inhabitants. www.census.gov/library/publications/1931/dec/1930a-vol-01-population.html.

US Census Bureau (2000). 2000 Census. www.census.gov/programs-surveys/decennial-census/decade/decennial-publications.2000.html.

US Census Bureau. 2021. Historical Income Tables. Historical Income Tables: Counties (census.gov). Accessed: March 25, 2022.

US. Climate Divisional Database. 2024. www.ncei.noaa.gov/access/monitoring/climate-at-a-glance/county/mapping. Accessed: March 25, 2022. www.ncei.noaa.gov/access/monitoring/climate-at-a-glance/divisional/mapping.

US Energy Information Administration. 2022. "Biomass Explained." www.eia.gov/energyexplained/biomass/. Accessed: March 27, 2022.

US Patent and Trademark Office. Patent Technology Monitoring Team (PTMT). 2022. www.uspto.gov/web/offices/ac/ido/oeip/taf/reports_cbsa.htm. Accessed: March 25, 2022.

US Trade Representative. 2021. "2021 Trade Policy Agenda and 2020 Annual Report of The President of The United States on the Trade Agreements Program." Online PDF 2021 Trade Policy Agenda and 2020 Annual Report.pdf (ustr.gov).

United States Patent and Trademark Office. 2000. *Technology Assessment and Forecast Report*. www.uspto.gov/web/offices/ac/ido/oeip/taf/county.pdf.

Varas, Antonio, and Raj Varadarajan. 2020. "How Restrictions to Trade with China Could End US Leadership in Semiconductors." *BCG Report* 9.

Viner, Jacob. 2016. *Studies in the Theory of International Trade*. New York: Routledge Press.

Waldorf, Brigitte, and Ayoung Kim. 2015. "Defining and Measuring Rurality in the US: From Typologies to Continuous Indices." In *Commissioned Manuscript*

Presented at the Workshop on Rationalizing Rural Area Classifications, Washington, DC.

Warf, Barney, and Mort Winsberg. 2008. "The Geography of Religious Diversity in the United States." *The Professional Geographer* 60(3): 413–424.

Weber, Lauren, Peter Grant, and Liz Hoffman. 2022. "Big Cities Can't Get Workers Back to the Office." *Wall Street Journal*. www.wsj.com/articles/office-remote-work-new-york-11657130765.

Williams, Joan C. 2017. *White Working Class: Overcoming Class Cluelessness in America*. Boston: Harvard Business Press.

Williams, Joan. 2020. "How Biden Won Back (Enough of) the White Working Class. *Harvard Business Review*. https://hbr.org/2020/11/how-biden-won-back-enough-of-the-white-working-class.

Wittstock, Nicolas. 2024. US Clean Energy Innovation-Fingerprints of the Military's Green Thumb. Working Paper. https://ssrn.com/abstract=4730197 or http://dx.doi.org/10.2139/ssrn.4730197.

Wei, Shang-Jin, and Yi Wu. 2001. "Globalization and Inequality: Evidence from within China." *National Bureau of Economic Research*. No. w8611.

Weiss, Linda. 2014. *America Inc.?: Innovation and Enterprise in the National Security State*. Cornell: Cornell University Press.

White House. 2021. Press Release. www.whitehouse.gov/briefing-room/statements-releases/2021/06/08/statement-of-president-joe-biden-on-senate-passage-of-the-u-s-innovation-and-competition-act/.

White House. 2023. "The Biden-Harris Administration's Investing in America Agenda: Delivering for Wisconsin." IIA-All-State-Fact-Sheets-Wisconsin.pdf (whitehouse.gov).

Williams, Joan. 2020. "How Biden Won Back (Enough of) the White Working Class. *Harvard Business Review*. https://hbr.org/2020/11/how-biden-won-back-enough-of-the-white-working-class.

Williams, Joan. 2019. *White Working Class: Overcoming Class Cluelessness in America*. Cambridge, MA: Harvard Business Press.

Wright, Gavin. 2020. "World War II, the Cold War, and the Knowledge Economies of the Pacific Coast." In *World War II and the West It Wrought*, eds., Mark Brilliant and David M. Kennedy. Stanford: Stanford University Press: 74–99.

Xu, Xu, Alison Watts, and Markum Reed. 2019. "Does Access to the Internet Promote Innovation? A Look at the US Broadband Industry." *Growth and Change* 50(4): 1423–1440.

Cambridge Elements

Law, Economics and Politics

Series Editor in Chief
Carmine Guerriero, *University of Bologna*

Series Co-Editors
Alessandro Riboni, *École Polytechnique*
Jillian Grennan, *Duke University, Fuqua School of Business*
Petros Sekeris, *TBS Education*

Series Managing Editor
Valentino Moscariello, *University of Bologna*

Series Associate Editors
Maija Halonen-Akatwijuka, *University of Bristol*
Sara Biancini, *Université de Cergy-Pontoise*
Melanie Meng Xue, *London School of Economics and Political Science*
Claire Lim, *Queen Mary University of London*
Andy Hanssen, *Clemson University*
Giacomo Benati, *Eberhard Karls University, Tübingen*

About the Series
Decisions taken by individuals are influenced by formal and informal institutions. Legal and political institutions determine the nature, scope and operation of markets, organisations and states. This interdisciplinary series analyses the functioning, determinants, and impact of these institutions, organizing the existing knowledge and guiding future research.

Cambridge Elements

Law, Economics and Politics

Elements in the Series

The Strategic Analysis of Judicial Behavior: A Comparative Perspective
Lee Epstein and Keren Weinshall

Can Blockchain Solve the Hold-up Problem in Contracts?
Richard Holden and Anup Malani

Deep IV in Law Appellate Decisions and Texts Impact Sentencing in Trial Courts
Zhe Huang, Xinyue Zhang, Ruofan Wang and Daniel L. Chen

Reform for Sale A Common Agency Model with Moral Hazard Frictions
Perrin Lefebvre and David Martimort

A Safety Valve Model of Equity as Anti-opportunism
Kenneth Ayotte, Ezra Friedman and Henry E. Smith

More Is Less: Why Parties May Deliberately Write Incomplete Contracts
Maija Halonen-Akatwijuka and Oliver Hart

US Innovation Inequality and Trumpism: The Political Economy of Technology Deserts in a Knowledge Economy
Victor Menaldo and Nicolas Wittstock

A full series listing is available at: www.cambridge.org/ELEP

For EU product safety concerns, contact us at Calle de José Abascal, 56–1°, 28003 Madrid, Spain or eugpsr@cambridge.org.

www.ingramcontent.com/pod-product-compliance
Lightning Source LLC
LaVergne TN
LVHW020332260326
834688LV00037B/990